Marjorie Parr

Chelsea and St Ives Art Dealer

Peter Davies

ISBN 978-1-905967-17-9

Published in the U.K. by
Old Bakehouse Publications
Church Street,
Abertillery, Gwent NP13 1EA
Telephone: 01495 212600
Fax: 01495 216222
Email: theoldbakeprint@btconnect.com
Website: www.oldbakehouseprint.co.uk

Made and printed in the UK
by J.R. Davies (Printers) Ltd.

British Library Cataloguing in Publication Data: a catalogue record for this book is available from the British Library.

also by the same author:

The St Ives Years, 1984

Art in Poole and Dorset, 1987

A Northern School, 1989

Josef Herman: Studies and Motifs, 1990

Liverpool Seen, 1992

St Ives Revisited, 1994

Arthur Ballard, 1996

Michael Kenny Sculpture, 1997

The Sculpture of John Milne, 2000

After Trewyn, 2001

Denis Bowen, 2001

Bratby, 2002

5 Devon Potters, 2004

John Huggins, 2006

St Ives 1975-2005: Art Colony in Transition, 2007

Contents

Alfred Hitchens 'Portrait of Marjorie Parr', c1926.
pencil and pastel.

Introduction
by Michael Shepherd

Every morning, painters, sculptors, mixed-media artists, unlock their studios and confront the work-in-progress of the previous day with fresh morning eyes... some to find continuation, some to scrap it all as unsatisfactory and start again. Many will confront the excitement or empty-mindedness of starting on a new work. Meanwhile others pack their recent work carefully into a small van, to take it off for the judgment of art dealers known or unknown, who will assess it in the light of saleability, and the artist's previous output. All this, a far cry from the 'private views' (anything but private, in the centre of town...) with their carefully-creamed-off works on immaculate walls under bright lights, refreshments and the glitterchatter of celebrities in their own eyes, establishing that this, here, now, is where it's at. What survives of all this activity, the art books and retrospective museum exhibitions tell us. But behind the 'works', the work : the human stories of the humming 'art world', which seldom get recorded.

So Peter Davies records for us one such story of the busy, enthusiastic, devoted, supportive, backroom of the art world : one woman, one gallery, and the network of support that artists - always simultaneously proud and unsure of their own work - require. And the more interesting a story in many ways, in that it tells of days not so long ago, when visual art was a minority interest in Britain - indeed, when the visual sense was barely developed in most Britons, compared with our word-oriented literary tradition : when artists really needed encouragement and a network of support.

In the late 1940s, a mere 60 years ago but another world it may seem now, the war in Europe had only just ended in 1945. To the eyes of anyone up from the countryside on the train, London looked drained; and so did most of its white-to-grey-faced citizens : Britain was thankful, optimistic, but drained. We'd won the war, but lost the peace. Hence the 1951 'Festival of Britain', with its bright primary colours set off by 'thames green', or sludge; its reminders of pre-war idealist architecture for the masses in Corbusian white concrete that stood little chance in Britain's not-yet-smokefree cities... and its hoped-for injection of euphoria. As for the small 'art world', experienced European connoisseurs of contemporary art such as Henri Roland, Gustave Delbanco, Erica Brausen, and a little later, Annely Juda and Andreas Kalman, set up art galleries in the West End and sold fine works for enviably small sums of money... and the few resident British who were already enthusiasts for art began to build up a support structure for the few artists who might hope to make a living from art or part-time art. One such support structure came from the fact that Britain, paradoxically, had more art schools than any other nation in Europe - something like 80 all told... (some nations had a bare 2...) So aspiring painters and a very few sculptors could just about survive on the proceeds of a few days a week's teaching in art schools.

Books on British artists were few too, in those days when 'Henry Moore' was still a standard term of abuse... just a few Penguin Modern Painters in a series that terminated... it would be the 1960s before Jasia Reichardt persuaded Methuen to produce a tiny set of books on such as Francis Bacon and Victor Pasmore... And the established 'Studio' magazine was still close to its craft-oriented roots. It was the publishing house Lund Humphries who set new standards and world-wide reputations when it moved from architecture to include fine books on Moore and Hepworth; while the British Council made Henry Moore its artistic ambassador. Around 1950, a retired doctor, Richard Gainsborough, founded a two-page fortnightly 'trade rag', 'Arts News and Review' (later 'Arts Review'), recording current art exhibitions in London. It was financed on a simple format : take a display advertising space, and we'll give you a review of the same size... but we won't promise that it will be a good review; just a fair review...

And that is where Peter Davies and I come in : we both cut our critical and even charitable teeth on Arts Review; as did most of the young writers and critics of the day. Peter and I shared an enthusiasm for meditation, which was still a freaky, fringy interest. Who now remembers the British Beats and their prized books on Zen and early Pacific Jazz records of such as Chet Baker, in the days before the happy hippies of the 1960s? Experimental lives in the 1950s in Britain took place behind closed doors. And so I and others set off from our paid jobs at lunchtimes, or at weekends, as we dived into those exciting basements or small rooms such as Denis Bowen's gallery, where youth was offering its raw new experiments in art. One stopping-off point for critics and patrons alike would be Marjorie Parr's gallery in Kings Road, where in civilised manner far from the aspirations of West End galleries - yet even more crucial to developing British artists - smaller paintings of quality would mix, as in a living-room, with furniture, pottery, and shelf-scale sculpture. And though most of us couldn't afford the time or the rail fare - we knew that St Ives, with its almost Mediterranean brightness of atmosphere, was a crucible for all painting, sculpture and studio pottery that rejoiced in light. It's difficult not to look back, some of us, with nostalgia, for a time when before television brought us a keener sense of the visual, art had to fight it's way onto walls and into hearts with the ardent support of such as Marjorie Parr. And hence, this admirable book by a writer who has happily continued to tell the tale of art as it emerges.

Michael Shepherd was 'Sunday Telegraph' Art Critic and Assistant Editor of 'Arts Review' during the 1970s and 1980s.

Chapter One

From Portobello to Kings Road 1960-67

Marjorie Parr was an art dealer and gallery owner of extraordinary vigour, charm and fortitude. The gallery she founded at 285 Kings Road, Chelsea in 1963 went on, during the next close-on 20 years, to host numerous exhibitions by young contemporary artists she believed in, and established British and continental modern masters often loaned from major West End galleries such as Waddington, the Mercury and Marlborough. A stylistc eclecticism, underpinned by catholic - sometimes even exotic or ethnic - taste, characterised the Marjorie Parr Gallery's exhibition policy. On a social level, too, her natural ability to get on with people instilled a welcoming atmosphere to the general public. As a result the gallery was visited by a wide range of people, among them students, tourists, passers-by, locals, artists and of course serious collectors and buyers.

The success of the enterprise was based on two fundamentals. What the Cornish painter, photographer, book illustrator and self-styled surrealist Andrew Lanyon later called Parr's "knack for selling"*1 went hand in hand with this much-loved gallerist's profound loyalty to her artists, with the courage to go on hunches and air new talent and with social ease and grace. This was clearly genuine, natural and infectious and won her a devoted following. During a pre-monetarist age when the business climate was perhaps kinder and less pressured than today Marjorie Parr championed artists with an innocent, pioneering zeal. By the same token she triumphed against the backdrop of a less developed gallery culture where art buying and collecting had not yet taken off and was restricted to old money or discerning middle class and professional coteries.

In a pre-yuppie, pre-internet age, then, she offered a broad aesthetic brush albeit one where certain prominent strands and traditions within modern and contemporary art stood out. Her allegiances to St Ives art, for example, led to what even today is the rare instance of a metropolitan gallery opening a regional branch. A second Marjorie Parr Gallery, at Will's Lane, St Ives operated between 1969 and 1971 and gave her full rein to promote an even broader range of Cornish artists than had already been the case on Kings Road.

A remarkable, possibly even unprecedented, feature of Marjorie Parr's art dealing career was that, having graduated from dealing in antiques and glass on the Portobello Road, she opened her Chelsea gallery at a mature age - she was a youthful 56 - when many are contemplating not-so-early retirement and exchanging the briefcase and bowler for the pipe and slippers. For this reason the painter John Hitchens described her as "everyone's favourite aunt",[*2] a tribute that rather than make her a child of the 1960s in fact turned her into a kind of maternal supporter of it. Her amenability to wide artistic variety chimed with the 'anything goes' ethos of swinging London in general and the 'groovy' Kings Road in particular. It was also symptomatic of a less populous gallery infrastructure where, unlike today, there was not the same need to specialise and create a niche market.

Marjorie Eileen Hidden was born on 21 December 1906 in Rugby, Warwickshire, the youngest of three children. Her father, a schoolteacher and musician, was the organist and choirmaster at St Andrew's Church. Marjorie's childhood ambition to be a ballet dancer was never realised due to her tall height. An Edwardian upbringing, though not unsympathetic, was a trifle stern and stultifying, her mother and elder sister Gwen both forceful and domineering, her banker brother Stan precise, conventional and finding Marjorie's expansive 'arty' character anathema. But the family background did exert the inadvertent, salutary effect of pushing her towards business and shopkeeping; in order to escape this background she married Samuel Goodman, a 'wholesale clothier', in Bromley, Kent in 1927. Furthermore Marjorie's penchant for the older man, perhaps replicated the father and elder brother figure of her upbringing (her father died when she was 12). Whatever the case the first of three marriages - to a man 33 years her senior - was crucial in that Goodman's links to the ragtrade undoubtedly encouraged Marjorie to open a dress shop in George Street, Hove where she cut her teeth as an entrepreneur and sales woman.

It also led, auspiciously, to an important early art world contact. One of her customers was Ethel, wife of Alfred Hitchens and mother of Ivon later to become one of the leading mid 20th century British landscape

8

Marjorie Parr, 1949.
Photo: Godfrey Coke.

painters. Marjorie became friendly with the Hitchens family, Alfred producing a competent, lightly coloured pencil portrait of Marjorie. Framed by Husseys near the dress shop, the drawing not only depicts Marjorie as a 'bright young thing' and something of an Art Deco age beauty but also as a steady, unflappable and quietly self-assured businesswoman. The marriage lasted 11 years and, barely a week after obtaining a divorce from Goodman, Marjorie married her second husband 43 year-old Geoffrey Tilley of Tilley Lamps in early July 1938 in St Pancras, London. Though slightly shorter in duration this 9-year marriage was happy and only ended due to Tilley's death in Northamptonshire in 1947 from a brain tumour.

Marjorie lived at Ibstone, Oxfordshire during the Tilley years. A friendship with the novelist Rebecca West, a near neighbour in Ibstone, developed during the early 1950s. West's affection for Marjorie was expressed in her correspondence, the troubled writer thanking Marjorie for a dinner party in February 1954 and telling her that "I always feel your sympathy and know that you are loyal and honest and that there's nothing but sweetness to come from you. I know what a terrible time you have and always hope that someone will do something to make the burden lighter".*³ That something came in the form of her third and final marriage to 60 year-old Samuel Parr in August 1954 at Hambledon, near Henley, Oxon. The burden West speaks of probably related to Marjorie's grief for Tilley, for looming financial worries and for her mother's last illness leading to her death shortly after in January 1955.

Sam Parr, her third husband, was Marjorie's senior, in his case by 13 years. They were together for barely 4 years, the final divorce in May 1960 citing complete incompatability. Attempts to save the marriage included a 6 month trip to South Africa during the winter of 1956-57. After separating, Marjorie moved to Old Bank House, Watlington, in Oxfordshire to join her nephew Basil Pollard. A small antique shop in Watlington proved a harbinger of things to come, the short-lived enterprise leading on to London's Portobello Road where she ran an indoor market stall each Saturday at Collectors Corner throughout the early 1960s. A trip to North America selling silverware on consignment gave her further sales experience. She moved into a flat in Lexham Gardens, Kensington during the Portobello years from which she traded by appointment in 18th century furniture, porcelain, silver and glass. The establishment of the Marjorie Parr Gallery on the Kings Road in 1963 and her move from Lexham Gardens to a new flat at Elm Park Gardens in July 1966, set the scene for the rest of her long and successful professional life.

When she acquired it, No. 285 Kings Road had been a shoe repair shop for 80 years. The basement, where she began showing fine art by selected artist friends to complement the main glass business, retained its original earth floor. While this was soon concreted over as part of major re-decorating, the basement was occasionally flooded. Jilly Knight, an early gallery assistant, (1964-67), remembered Marjorie being "pretty knowledgeable" on antique glass but "wasn't so interested"*4 in furniture. Among the stock of over 300 glass items were wine glasses, drawn trumpets and other 18th century objects. Sidney Crompton, a glass expert who edited the Ward Lock book 'English Glass' (1967), rented a top floor room and bought his knowledge to bear, using an X-Ray machine to detect soda or lead components in respective glass objects. She also let the first floor to Roger and Sue Patterson who needed office space; Patterson's father collected glass.

Parr was always, as Knight recalled, "highly organised", and was "good at hanging pictures" from an early stage. This was important because the mixed show was often a mêlée containing not only fleeting and incidental, but also recurring, names who would come to fill the solo exhibition schedule during the next 15 years. These included the painters John Hitchens and Guy Worsdell, the latter having the new gallery's maiden show, and the sculptors Peter Ball, Peter Thursby, Margaret Lovell, Jill Tweed and Roger Leigh who appeared during the gallery's early days between 1963 and 1965. But in terms of mixed displays the gallery also presented artists like Michael Andrews who, despite being a mere 19 year-old in 1964, impressed Susan Groom with his "remarkable

Marjorie Parr with the Earl of Mount Edgcumbe and Peter Thursby at Thursby's exhibition opening City Art Gallery, Plymouth, February 1964.
Photo: Western Morning News.

maturity".*5 Other exhibitors like the two Julias, Davidson and de Meric, proved ships in the night. Peter Ball, on the other hand, who accompanied these painters in a mixed high summer show in August 1964, would become a gallery fixture in the coming years. Groom observed, perhaps rather obviously, that through neo-primitive figures Ball was "trying to imbue... the hieratic and timeless qualities of African sculpture".

This ethnicity and anthropomorphism, reflecting a strand of the gallery's taste in the coming years, contrasted with the modern formalism of Peter Thursby's metamorphic machines. Thursby's solo exhibition 'Sculpture and Drawings' in September witnessed "several changes of style" that were however "linked by an obsessive concern for texture"*6 according to Oswell Blakeston. The reviewer preferred a series of 'Winged Creatures' and small painted machine forms to other pieces felt by Blakeston to have "neglected study of form... in pursuit of surface qualities." Notwithstanding Thursby's convincing large scale painting 'oeuvre', the work of a lyrical landscape painter - namely John Hitchens - inspired by South Downs topographicality - was always going to register a different outcome both in a visual and commercial sense.

Hitchens' maiden Marjorie Parr exhibition 'Sussex Landscapes' in October 1964 contained 30 pictures many of which concerned themselves with the movement of clouds or vicissitudes of light and weather against hilltops. Typical examples like 'Hills and Summer Clouds', 'South Downs under South West Clouds' and 'Lowlands with Moving Clouds' led Susan Groom to describe an artist who "employs a vast range of feelings, and captures every mood of the Sussex landscape... a feeling of a high wind and speed".*7 Groom felt that while Hitchens' "swiftly applied brush strokes are a little inadequate.." they nevertheless contained a "swiftness of touch that gives them their power." The distinguished critic Eric Newton took to exploring what he described as "the superficial similarity and a less superficial difference"*8 between the work of father and son. "The similarity is one of method," Newton continued, "for both use a broad

John Hitchens 'Duncton Down in Shadow', 1964.
oil.

brushstroke, both use it with a controlled swiftness that looks easy but only arrives after a good deal more trial than error, and both have a lot of white canvas uncovered which not only gives it a sparkle but almost uncannily suggests light and space". Newton described the differences as "one of mood... while Ivon Hitchens is a temperamental romantic in the line from Turner John, taking his inspiration from Constable, focuses on gently rolling hills, flashing foliage and the tumult of English clouds".

Guy Worsdell re-appeared in May 1965, Groom describing a "shadowy, ghost-like quality" to "romantic abstracts".*9 Margaret Lovell too, whose exhibition followed Worsdell's in June, seemed to invest an abstract, or at least formal, language with suggestions of the natural or organic. Groom summarised Lovell's tall, slim upright bronzes as "definitely classical: static, simple and seeking the essential order behind the apparent chaos of the world around".*10 Describing the exhibition as "full and absorbing" Groom countenanced what would become a long and successful relationship between sculptor and gallerist. Peter Thursby, on the other hand - though a pioneering artist at the gallery - found less commercial success with his industrial vision using pipes, metal offcuts and other mechanical elements. Despite this Groom was able to report on an Exeter-based sculptor who "has defined and refined his ideas to produce a worthwhile body of work".*11 Thursby's friend, the architect-trained sculptor Roger Leigh (1925-1997), one-time Barbara Hepworth studio assistant who later lodged with Thursby during teaching stints at Exeter College of Art, bridged the gap between the organic and the industrial - or in his case the architectural - worlds in terms of cantilevered wood constructions like 'Annular Fracture' (1963) and 'Walk Knot' (1964).

Roger Leigh 'Annular Fracture', 1963. wood.

A slightly larger Hitchens exhibition (33 pictures) than in 1964 took place in November. 'Land Sea Sky' was accompanied by a smart four-page crimson card though the blank back cover may more profitably have contained a critical or promotional essay. Lawrence Bradshaw and T.G. Rosenthal, writing in 'Arts Review' and 'The Listener' respectively, partially made up for this and echoed the previous commentaries of Groom and Newton, Bradshaw describing "vast panoramas of cumulus clouds, sweeping low over the horizon",*12 Rosenthal stating that Hitchens junior had "inherited a masterly economy of means... so that his Sussex fields and coastline under rain and sun and storm take on a cool but sensual beauty".*13 Using a gesturally assertive language of brushwork inherited from Ivon, John produced for this show pictures like 'Corn Light', 'Ebbtide Reach', 'Landscape after Rain', 'Towering Cloud Masses' and 'Coastal Evening' that positively evoked, a la Vivian Pitchforth, a fecund, verdant, atmospheric English landscape vision.

Robert Clatworthy 'Bull'.
bronze.
courtesy Keith Chapman.

Marjorie's "knack for selling" found perfect outlet in the end-of-the-year pot-pourri of small works intended as Christmas gifts. This provided the theme of a December 1965 show the eclecticism of which the reviewer Joanna Borchand described in terms of having "really not much in common except the lowness of the prices. Apart from a notable absence of any kinetic art, almost all styles are included in 3 well-crammed rooms".[14] Borchand went on to single out an "exceptionally pleasing" watercolour drawing of a soldier's head by Elisabeth Frink, Kate Nicholson's "far from tentative" picture 'Shining Word' and "a wall of exciting primitives by John Christopherson and Gillian Beccles". And while Marjorie would indeed continue to use the large group show throughout many yule times to come she did not limit the tempting displays of cheaper work to the end of the year.

Parr started 1966, for example, with a group exhibition in January, a display of sculpture by 17 artists in February and a spring show including Patrick Hall and John Hitchens during April. The former contained now unfamiliar names that have not lasted; nonetheless Michael Greary, whose 'Standing Figure' series dominated downstairs, was described by Bradshaw as "a strong, uncompromising young painter"[15] while Daphne Reynolds' whimsy and the abstracts of Dorothy Alexander and Herbert Harrison were given favourable notice. One artist to stand the test of time, Kate Nicholson, was featured with "delicate and restrained but dynamic" paintings. The same discrete mastery of form to accomodate dynamic and lyrical qualities invested the next exhibition of small, mainly bronze, sculpture with "a range of interest and excellence"[16] in the eyes of Cottie Burland. Robert Clatworthy's 'Bull', for example, registered lively surface modelling that Burland wrote "united form with movement." Equally, Henry Moore's 'Upright Motif' was described as "a totem pole of human life". The expressively simplified bronze 'Head' by Marcia Panama and Margaret Lovell's enigmatic 'Box on Tripod Legs' did not project movement directly so much as suggest the passage of time. The 'Kensington Post' felt Parr to be "a strong woman with strong views, which have paid off".[17]

Evident here - at an early stage in the gallery's history - was the blending of established names from the older (Moore) and middle generations (Clatworthy, Oliffe Richmond and Frink) with younger sculptors. These included both Panama and Lovell and other 1966 debutants Mark Ingram and June Barrington-Ward. While establishing principles, one of which was the winning combination of youth and experience, Marjorie continued the sale of glass and small antiques. This familiar activity was an insurance policy until her fully fledged and redesigned art gallery opened in February 1970.

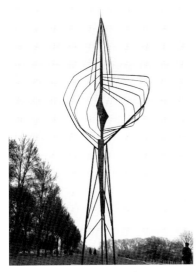

June Barrington-Ward 'Elemental Form'.
welded steel.

Chapter Two

Swinging with the Sixties 1967-69

Enjoying a third solo Parr exhibition, comprising an unprecedented 35 paintings, John Hitchens consolidated an important ongoing relationship with the gallery. Paintings like 'Sea Wind', 'Storm Charged Hills', 'Sand diffused with Sea' and 'White Shore' demonstrated both the prevalence of elemental flux and climatic vicissitude within Hitchens' landscape vision and also the establishment of pertinent variations from Ivon's still looming influence. Following Eric Newton's earlier detection of a salient divergence between the work of father and son at John's maiden exhibition with Marjorie Parr in 1964 the 'Chelsea Post' reviewer wrote that John "already showed the style and mood of his father but as the years have passed his own personal pattern is developing." John's preceived readiness to embrace broader topography and landscape vistas, away from the enclosed woodland with shrouded ponds favoured by Ivon, was also noted by Susan Groom - along with Newton a reviewer of the 1964 show - now wrote of the younger man having "reached a new height in clarity and freshness... there is also more detail, casual but sure".[1]

The gallery's association with John Hitchens represented lyrical landscape abstraction based on a quintessentially English feeling for 'genius loci'. Parr's allegiance to St Ives - soon to be realised with the opening of a second gallery, in St Ives, in 1969 - continued such interests, while allowing her personal taste for the applied and decorative arts to become an equally prominent aspect of gallery policy. This was natural for a dealer whose roots lay not in fine art but in the furniture and glass trade. The renowned Cornish art colony's association with creative studio pottery, furniture-making and even jewellery provided Parr with options beyond mainstream painting or sculpture. In May 1967, for example, the polymath Breon O'Casey exhibited 38 paintings and reliefs in characteristic sombre, rich or bright colour, informed by the parallel creative activities of jewellery-making, textile designing and sculpture-making, alongside recent bronzes (1960-65) by his friend Denis Mitchell. The strong craftsmanly cult of making refined objects with hands had been instilled in both artists through their respective employment during the 1950s in Barbara Hepworth's Trewyn Studio in the heart of St Ives.

Mitchell, the longer serving Hepworth assistant (1949-60), developed a slim, predominantly upright, repertoire of polished or patinated bronze forms influenced both by carving sections of wood or stone to Hepworth's designs and by his former employment

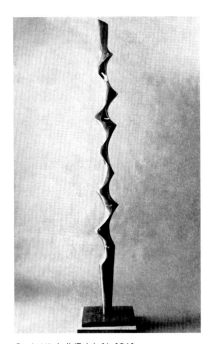

Denis Mitchell 'Zelah 1', 1961.
bronze.

as agrarian labourer, fisherman and tin miner. The spiralling corkscrew or hook-like shapes of the bronzes that followed a first cast work 'Zawn' (1958) reflected the implements of both an artisanal past and an artistic present. 'Zelah 1' (1961) and 'Zelah 11' (1963) in polished bronze and aluminium bronze respectively, reflected the miner's drill while announcing the artist's meticulous and painstaking rendering of rough foundry casts through laborious filing, chiselling and polishing. The results were contemplative objects of poise and beauty, self-contained yet open to their surroundings in terms of mirrored distortions. A use of 'U' shaped cavities between pairs of forked upright forms characterised other early 1960s bronzes like 'Porthcressa' (1961) or 'Clowance' (1964). The financially precarious years of the early 1960s - between leaving Trewyn Studio and becoming a full-time sculptor in 1967 - were alleviated by solo exhibitions at Waddington, London (1961), Devorah Sherman, Chicago, Redfern, London (1962), Bianchini, New York (1963) and finally at Arnolfini, Bristol. No doubt due to Parr, 'Porthcressa' entered the Arts Council collection in 1969.

O'Casey's titles for the 1967 exhibition with Mitchell, among them 'Blue Diamond', 'Brown Undulation' and 'Blue Bar Through Green' revealed the primary structural, as well as emotional, role of colour within simple, even minimal, formats. The shapes were perhaps the outcome of fashioning hard materials like wood, stone or metal in his capacity as Hepworth assistant and jewellery-maker. Form and colour merged in these works in a manner championed at this time by colour field, minimal and post painterly abstraction. His work was, however, less a product of metropolitan abstraction than of a St Ives tradition of handicraft where ethnic, pagan symbolism invested 'pure', reduced form with anthropomorphic significance. While the installation's chaotic and cluttered setting alongside antique furniture chimed with H.S. Ede's vision of domestic informality at Kettles' Yard, Cambridge it offered little in the way of a coherent, visually neutral context. The detached and clinical context needed to see the work clearly would await the new revamped space with which this increasingly popular gallery ushered in the 1970s.

The so-called 'flower power' summer of love (1967) saw the gallery reflect Marjorie's interest in the applied arts and her natural, outgoing social inclusiveness. Beads and kaftans were as welcome as collars and ties, an engaging dealer talking to all comers at face value. An exhibition in July of studio pottery by Janet Leach and Catherine Yarrow was followed in August by a blockbuster exhibition, appropriately and pertinently on the theme of floral still life, that included the work of Duncan Grant, Winifred Nicholson, Rowland Suddaby, Jean

Catherine Yarrow 'Tower', c1966.
stoneware.
Photo: Anthony Shaw.

Marchand and 'younger' contemporaries like Patrick Hall, John Hitchens and Phillipa Denby. A diverse and historically eclectic range was linked around a single coherent context, flower painting. Colourism and a relish for paint and gesture also characterised much of the exhibition giving it an expressive and lyrical breadth.

An exhibition of Guy Worsdell paintings and Michael Rothenstein prints in October proved the exception to sculpture displays that dominated the gallery throughout the autumn. Nowhere was Parr's even-handedness between the abstract and figurative currents of modern sculpture more in evidence than in a September exhibition of the Barnes-based husband and wife team Philip Hicks and Jill Tweed. Hicks' two dozen metal reliefs, accompanied by paintings, were deemed by 'Arts Review' "to form a modern mythology',*2 emulating Paolozzi's interplay between primitive and modern industrial form.

Hicks' cold cast aluminium reliefs conveyed formal and architectonic, rather than anthropomorphic, intentions. Hicks later described his work in "a transitional state"*3 where pure form, detached from colour, could be explored. Containing ambiguity and spatial tension between pictorial (form in plan) and sculptural (form in elevation) orientations these works also represented an artist in the throes of exchanging painted marine or landscape imagery for urban, architectural iconography. Later, the Imperial War Museum acquired a series of shaped wood or metal reliefs, dubbed the 'Vietnam Requiem' produced in memory of Philip's soldier father. The reliefs, in relating to the shaped canvases of contemporary hard edge and minimal modes, allied formalism with military symbolism.

Philip Hicks and Jill Tweed exhibition, September 1967. Tweed's head of Alan Freeman is on the furniture.

Jill Tweed, whose bronze 'Fighting Bird' was sold by Parr as early as 1965, benefited from portrait commissions put in her way by a dynamic and socially interactive dealer; these included busts of the children of notables like the managing director of Austin Reed, or of the left-wing Hollywood film director Carl Foreman. A resin portrait of popular radio DJ Alan Freeman produced from life in Tweed's King's Road studio in March 1965 was shown in the September 1967 exhibition alongside portrait busts and trademark bird pieces. Tweed's penchant for dog, bird or horse subjects - invariably in animated or moving poses - both owed a debt to her friend Elisabeth Frink through whom she met Marjorie, and later proved influential on the work of her celebrated sculptor daughter Nicola (b.1960). The influence of F.E. McWilliam, her Slade tutor, Frink and Germaine Richier engendered an expressive, even distorted, treatment of animals quite removed from the neater equestrian, goat or standing proletarian or military subjects commissioned during the 1990s and beyond, in Hampshire and Gloucestershire. Like her mother Catherine Tweed, a Slade-trained portrait painter who received a Royal commission (pastel portraits of Princes Edward and Andrew), Jill always struck an immediate and telling likeness. Although Hicks and Tweed moved on - the former going on to show with the New Arts Centre and David Messum the latter with Jonathan Poole and the Bruton Street Gallery - they kept in touch with Marjorie. She responded to exhibition notices with a good luck card.

Parr had learnt the trick of offering small, mantlepiece sculpture by notable modern sculptors, whether abstract or figurative, for Christmas. The year 1967 was seen out with such an exhibition whose stylistically broad and inclusive range was noted by the 'Arts Review' founder Richard Gainsborough's son, John, who described the traditionalism of Plazzotta at one end of the aesthetic spectrum and "the abstract purity of form"*4 of Tessier and others at the other. Norbert Lynton in the 'Guardian' noted that "it is a tempting exhibition for those crazy enough to think of giving art as Christmas presents instead of keeping it themselves, though it takes a confident sculpture to compete with the antique furniture they also sell."*5 Robert Adams, F.E. McWilliam, Elisabeth Frink, Denis Mitchell, Margaret Lovell, Adam Tessier, Paul Bridgeman, Friederich Werthmann and Plazzotta epitomised the broad aesthetic spectrum, Mitchell and Lovell representing a Hepworth-influenced abstract classicism, McWilliam surreal distortion, Frink figurative expressionism, Adams neo-constructivist geometry, Plazzotta mythological symbolism and Werthmann's 'La Suite' welded steel lyricism.

Friederich Werthmann 'La Suite', 1966.
stainless steel.
Photo: Sheila Sorley.

This commercially astute sculpture exhibition was matched, early in 1968, by a 'Small Paintings' display

17

Sculpture by Peter Thursby and June
Barrington-Ward in the snowy courtyard.
Photo: Mary Lambert.

among which were two Patrick Heron gouaches in which bright, informal blobs of colour bled into one another, trademark John Hitchens Sussex landscapes and small Thetis Blackers whose "dream generated themes" seemed to Richard Walker to be "realised with exquiste wide-awake exactitude".*5 This observation highlighted a contradiction within romantic and surrealist art, namely the use of paradoxically objective technique and high finish to articulate outlandish or subjectively obscure imagery. Walker, however claimed there was "nothing to sustain an appetite for ugliness or vulgarity" at a gallery where it was felt refined taste and social good grace prevailed.

Parr on occasion turned to the established West End dealer Leslie Waddington from whom she loaned works by Ivon Hitchens, Patrick Hall or Henri Hayden. A small exhibition of works by Hayden in February followed a larger solo Hayden show at Waddingtons the previous summer. The French modern master - perhaps 'petit maitre' would be an apter description - was followed by an altogether different gathering on the Kings Road in March and April. A contemporary group exhibition focused on the staff and students of Edinburgh College of Art. Featuring the work of two generations, the exhibition revealed Scottish art's links to the French colour and lyric tradition of which Hayden was a representative. The display now seems problematic in that work by Elizabeth Blackadder, John Houston, David Michie, Denis Peploe and Robin Philipson has stood the test of time, while that of the students has fallen into anonymity, the class of '68 not enjoying the later acclaim of the 1980s generation, Conroy, Campbell, Howson, et al, that emerged from Edinburgh and Glasgow.

David Michie 'Joe's Fritter Fry'.
oil.

Marjorie's even-handedness extended beyond the abstract v figurative issue to embrace studio ceramics which was seen as standing on equal creative footing with fine art, Unlike many art dealers before or since she did not relegate sculpture in order to concentrate on the decoratively easier soft option of painting. On the contrary, one of the few notes of discontent from her stock of artists came from the painter, Breon O'Casey, who harboured long term resentment at what be saw as his subordination to the sculptor John Milne (O'Casey was given an upper floor and Milne the more prominent ground, street level floor) in a two-person show in 1972.

In June 1968 the gallery accommodated Margaret Lovell's new sculpture. The exhibition was timely, Bristol's College Green and the ruins of Coventry's old cathedral dedicated to publically prominent outdoor displays of contemporary work by leading British sculptors. Lovell's show was also hugely successful. The Lovell exhibition extended to 42 pieces, mainly bronze though including marble, stone, alabaster and slate. Through these diverse materials and the

Margaret Lovell with 'Spinnaker', 1968. bronze.

disciplines of their fashioning, Lovell revealed a simplicity of conception linked to refinement of execution. It proved her most successful exhibition, before or since, with several editioned bronzes completely selling out. Four examples of 'Filloma' (edition 6), five of 'Spinnaker' (ed 6), four of 'Pantemenos' (ed 6), six of 'Juliet Head' (ed 9), two of 'Head' (ed 3) and three of 'Bird Movement' 9 (ed 3) sold. Carved pieces like 'Marinoid' (alabaster), 'Aurisina' (slate) and 'Elenitsa' (stone) also sold. The future owner of Marjorie's gallery, David Gilbert acquired the unique cast 'Barquentine', a regular gallery patron Derek Turner purchased 'Marinoid' and Nancy Balfour, later prominent in the Contemporary Art Society and other art bodies, bought 'Filloma'. A copy of the Hepworth-like editioned bronze 'Figalia' went to Stanley Picker and is now housed in the Stanley Picker collection in Kingston.

A pair of experimental works in the gallery backyard display area - where Marjorie was in the habit of throwing tea parties or informal coffee breaks - did not, however sell. The tautly linear abstract design of 'Relief Wall', carved in assembled thermolite blocks, originated from one of the designs for a stillborn commission from the TSB, Bristol. When this never materialised Lovell exhibited the ensuing structure at Parr's in the hope that an institutional buyer would commission a metal version for an architectural façade. It ended up in an entirely different context adorning the wall of an agricultural outbuilding at a farm outside Bath where Lovell lived with her first husband during the 1970s. A coloured glass window (Dec 1967), an exercise in loosely collaged colour fragments, remained with the artist after the successful 1968 exhibition.

The long-running saga of the proposed commission for the Great Ouse Water Authority, Huntingdon, did, though, finally see the light of day, Lovell receiving the go-ahead to produce a large 12 foot version of the 20 inch bronze 'Spinnaker' included in the 1968 show. Illustrated in David Clemens' 'Daily Mirror' feature 'Spinnaker' vindicated Clemens' claim that Lovell "looks like becoming one of Britain's most popular young artists".[6]

The contrasting Lovell and Enzo Plazzotta exhibitions in June and October respectively were divided between a regulation high summer season slot of gallery artists - modern master and contemporary alike - and a sizeable Kate Nicholson exhibition featuring 50 works during the favourable back-to-business month of September. The second of three Kate Nicholson solos, this exhibition again revealed Parr's links with Waddington, to whose gallery the talented offspring of Ben Nicholson's first marriage, to painter Winifred, had moved. Corsham-trained and

Kate and Winifred Nicholson in the gallery courtyard, September 1968.
Photo: Mary Lambert.

Enzo Plazzotta 'Hiroshima', 1968. bronze.

spending time after 1957 at St Ives, where she would keep a second home to complement her base at her mother's family home 'Bankshead' in Cumbria, Kate pursued a faux naif style indebted in various degrees to Ben's relaxed early style and to Winifred's almost mystical colourism. Kate's St Ives life was however blighted by the misfortunate timing of Ben's permanent move to Switzerland in 1958.

In common with that of Jill Tweed the sculpture of Enzo Plazzotta used human or animal form in animated movement. The particular theme of ballet provided Plazzotta with what Max Wykes-Joyce later described as "the ideal medium in which to develop an interest, discernible throughout his work, in the motive vigour of the human body".[7] Like Degas, therefore, Plazzotta used dance as a means of testing the structural versatility of stretched posture. Born in 1921 near Venice and taught under Giacomo Manzu in Milan, Plazzotta nonetheless spent most of his professional life in England despite keeping a second home near the Carrara marble quarries in northern Italy. He worked in a Chelsea studio formerly used by Royal Academy President Sir Charles Wheeler.

Wykes-Joyce observed that "Plazzotta was, by education and temperament, supremely a sculptor in

Enzo Plazzotta 'Peter Ustinov', 1968. bronze.

20

the Italian mould", the work exuding a meretricious classicism able to relay romantic content. He proved a popular seller, gallery breadwinner even, and instilled a note of academic convention at a time when abstraction was in the ascendent. Criticised in some quarters for possessing anachronistic elitism Plazzotta's work explored pertinent themes derived from myth, metaphor and modern symbolism. 'Hiroshima' and a multiple portrait of actor Peter Ustinov from this exhibition, for example, revealed how the sculptor could contribute to a late 1960s antiwar zeitgeist and also produce an instantly and universally recognisable portrait.

Appropriately Oswell Blakeston's review was illustrated with a bronze of ballerina Nadia Nerina.*[8] The following February, to mark her retirement from the Royal Ballet, the 'Daily Telegraph' gave a front page illustration of Nerina flanked by a Plazzotta

Enzo Plazzotta 'Nadia Nerina - Arabesque 1', 1967. bronze.

bronze. Similarly 'The Times' illustrated 'Camargue Horses' (1969) exhibited at Stowe School, Buckingham during summer 1969. Another from the bronze edition was later installed at the Barbican. These pieces demonstrated Plazzotta's animated, all round skill with modelling.

The Plazzotta was followed throughout November by a fourth solo John Hitchens exhibition, his largest to date, comprising 40 new paintings. The younger Hitchens had become a gallery stalwart, enjoying a

John Hitchens and family with Marjorie Parr, 1972.

workable, even enjoyable, artist-dealer relationship. Marjorie's old friendship with the Hitchens family, extending back three generations, put this relationship on a solid social, as well as business footing. Marjorie visited Ivon in Petworth buying paintings that augmented the more frequent loans from Waddington. Her recognition and nurturing of John's talent complemented Ivon's encouragement which John remembered oscillated between paternal pride at the son's unfolding career and the need to offer warnings about the hazards - financial, creative or otherwise - of the younger artist's chosen path.

A spirit of independence had indeed been with John since student days at Corsham, near Bath, where he seemed untouched by tutors of the magnitude of Adrian Heath, Howard Hodgkin or Malcolm Hughes. Recognising who he was they probably left him to his gestural, pastoral, coloristic devices. Though strikingly apparent, the influence of Ivon was a positive factor, one that John was able to discretely transcend. Experiments into first matter painting using uniform sand surfaces and later into ethnically-inspired shaped canvases and finally free-standing 'paintings' on carved trunks of wood revealed an artist on the move. Even within the abstracted trademark landscapes of the 1960s Hitchens was changing things, the 1968

John Hitchens 'Far Hills in Light', 1968. oil.

show exchanging site-specific topography for a new ethereality focused on weather and elemental flux achieved in terms of freer brushwork and atmospheric colour. Informed ultimately by Turner and Constable these atmospheric compositions bore axiomatic titles like 'Far Hills in Light', 'Yellow Evening Light', 'Blue Mists' and 'Sea Light Breaking'.

Another small but expedient end-of-year sculpture exhibition provided seasonal cheer for mantlepiece and window sill; it was also a prelude to a major Denis Mitchell exhibition in January 1969 (nearly 30 mainly bronze sculptures with 15 oils on gesso and 7 slate reliefs). Post -1967 sculpture, in accounting for half the exhibition, reflected a new energy and vindicated the decision to sculpt full time. To that end Mitchell had moved into an old schoolhouse studio, 'Trewarveneth', in Newlyn owned by his colleague and longstanding friend John Wells. In 1969, aided by commercial success with Marjorie Parr, the Mitchells moved from St Ives into a grand Cornish house 'La Pieta' near the top of Paul Hill in Newlyn. Mitchell owed much to the gallery, therefore, demonstrating his gratitude with a note of thanks inscribed in his catalogue.

The accompanying catalogue, which illustrated 'Zelah 1' (1961) as the frontispiece, contained a written endorsement by painter and critic Patrick Heron. Heron noted Mitchell's unfashionable adherence to carving. "Mitchell is the only important British sculptor, junior to Moore and Hepworth," Heron wrote "who has never deserted the carved or hand cut form as the sole vehicle of expression... sheer persistence has generated great quality." By "great quality" Heron meant masterly manual technique, a virtue he would increasingly identify as British or

Marjorie Parr with Denis Mitchell (right) and Chris Booth, February 1969. Photo: Mary Lambert.

European in his growing polemic against the American art world. The exhibition demonstrated the importance of carving streamlined, clean-cut forms from metal or wood. Among the latter was the lignum vitae 'Carnelloe' (1968) which would later be replicated into a zigzagging upright bronze (1975).

The critics John Russell and Edwin Mullins declared "perfected and shining surfaces" and "sharp, elegant sculpture" in the 'Sunday Times' and 'Sunday Telegraph' respectively.*⁹ Recent bronzes like 'Solaris', 'Nanquidno', 'Kerris' and 'Gorran' (1968) balanced symmetry with a feeling of unpredictable or precarious movement and highlighted contrasting exterior and interior surface through an intriguing interplay between gleaming polish and opaque verdigris. This critical exposure and commercial success gave Mitchell

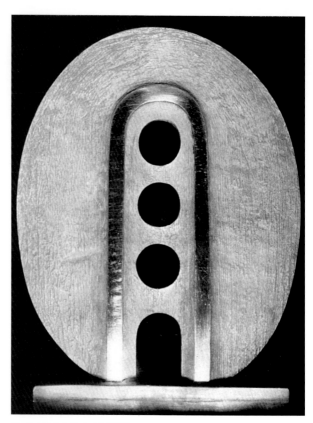

Denis Mitchell 'Solaris', 1968.
bronze.

confidence, the sculptor going on to make a lecture
tour of Colombia (1970), to enjoy another successful
Parr solo (1971) and to become a Governor of
Plymouth College of Art (1973).

Chapter Three

Parr For Two Courses 1969-71

The Mitchell exhibition was a reminder of the increasing importance of the St Ives artists to the Marjorie Parr enterprise. In mid May 1968 she wrote to Peter Thursby, one of the gallery's earliest sculptors, about the recent acquisition from Bill Wood of a small property called 'The Old Cottage Shop (Antiques)' at Will's Lane, St Ives. A day earlier Barbara Hepworth

from
DAME BARBARA HEPWORTH D.B.E.   13th. May, 1968.

Miss Marjorie Parr,
Marjorie Parr Galleries,
285 Kings Road,
Chelsea,
London, S.W.3.

My Dear Marjorie,

Thank you for both your letters. I am completely
delighted with the news.

I have looked at the place recently, praying that a
guardian angel would arrive and save it; and the fact
that you have acquired it now will mean so very much
to all of us. I cannot tell you how much!

It really was a great delight to see you and to get
to know you, and I was so grateful for the opportunity
and for all your kindness. I was also overwhelmed to
hear about the sculpture.

I hope now, perhaps we shall be able to meet quite often.

With very much love,

Barbara

wrote to Marjorie about being "completely delighted by the news".*1 A branch of the Marjorie Parr Gallery in St Ives would however have to wait almost a year, finally opening on April 2nd 1969. A celebratory dinner at the Outrigger Restaurant followed, an event that symbolised how "her friendship with painters was developing" in the eyes of the local 'St Ives Times and Echo'. But Marjorie also courted the public, the paper reporting that "she wanted to make her gallery a centre of ever-changing interest, not only to artists, but to St Ives people generally".*2

Outrigger Restaurant from left to right: Ivaldo Ferrari, Boots Redgrave, Brian Smith, Doreen O'Casey, Michael Truscott, Caroline Portway, John Milne, Sybil Hanson, Denis Mitchell and Marjorie Parr.

Marjorie Parr (centre) with Guy Worsdell, Sybil Hanson and Barbara Hepworth, Will's Lane, April 1969.

Douglas Portway (left) with Breon O'Casey.

John Milne (left) with Betty Holman and Brian Smith.

Guy Worsdell with Doreen O'Casey, Denis Mitchell, Eric Gibbard and Ivaldo Ferrari.

Bill Wood, Debbie and Michael Truscott, Will's Lane, 1969.

An integral part of this aim was, as we have seen, a pursuit of H.S. Ede's domestic vision in Cambridge; she told the 'Times and Echo' that "I show pictures, small sculptures and pottery on, or in relation to, furniture and furnishings rather than display them under spotlights, as in an exhibition... I try to show people how they can be lived with and enjoyed." The paper, in declaring a fortnight after the gallery's opening that "it is the only private gallery of modern art of its size and scope in west Cornwall and probably the only one west of Plymouth" revealed just how much has changed since then and pointed to Parr as a pioneering 'missionary' in the growth of the

Barbara Hepworth sculpture with Bernard Leach Pots, Will's Lane.

south-west Cornwall art gallery scene. The gallery interior was designed by the painter and architect John Miller whose elegantly reduced, sublimely coloured marine pictures and background as an ecclesiastical architectural designer ensured that it formed a sympathetic environment for modern art.

While representing the work of a ready-made stable of local Cornish artists the gallery also introduced artists from the Chelsea gallery. For the next

Vivien ap Rhys Pryce 'The John Player Sunday League Cricket Trophy', 1969. bronze.

two years the two galleries presented a remarkably coherent interplay between London and St Ives. This proved mutually beneficial with Marjorie able to promulgate contemporary Cornish artists in London and metropolitan artists in St Ives. Through the medium of the group show the gallery also presented artists of substance, like Roy Conn and Bob Crossley, who did not have solo exhibitions at either venue but nevertheless displayed work in intermittent group shows.

While much preoccupied with the opening of the St Ives gallery Parr showed in March three contrasting artists, Vivien ap Rhys Pryce, Pier Steensma and F.G. Hughes on the Kings Road. Barbara Wright in 'Arts Review' explained that "No words can praise this exhibition too highly",[3] The bronze figures of dancers by Rhys Pryce were deemed "in the true humanist tradition", thereby chiming - in spirit if not style - with the gouaches, woodcuts and oils on the theme of Buddhist monkhood by Steensma. This contemplative artist, who lived in Nepal for three years, produced simplified figures of monks glowing with a 'spiritual' quality of colour, predominantly scarlet and white. The theme of purity and essentialism translated in absolute and formal terms in the Gabo-inspired geometric perspex constructions of Hughes whose work Wright described as "exquisite".

Coinciding with the opening of the St Ives branch the exhibition 'Modern Paintings, Sculpture and Pots' in London that April fell back on an easily assembled group of gallery regulars among whom Michael Nye, the reviewer, singled out John Hitchens and Douglas Portway. What Nye termed Portway's "cool but energetic" semi abstract style enlivened the basement gallery which hosted a kind of low key solo. Overall, however, Nye detected an over decorative manner for "few of the paintings involve one at a very deep level".[4] The sculpture, on the other hand, which included the abstraction of Mitchell, Lovell and Milne in marked contrast to the figurative classicism of Plazzotta, was felt to be "of a different order, though of comparable heterogeneity." Pots by Bernard and Janet Leach and Lucie Rie established a real twain between SW3 and the Cornish Riviera.

An exhibition in May of paintings by the Edinburgh-trained Scottish artist James Cumming (1922-1991) proved that Marjorie's hand stretched not only from London to the far south-west but also from London to the north of Scotland, Cumming including 'The Hebridean' and 'The Lewis Poacher', now in the Fleming collection, and 'Gemete' among his 42 paintings. The Scottish connection was reinforced on the upper floor with works by the Edinburgh colleagues David Michie and Robin Philipson, an echo of the earlier show given to staff

Vivien ap Rhys Pryce 'Jazz Dancer', 1970. bronze.

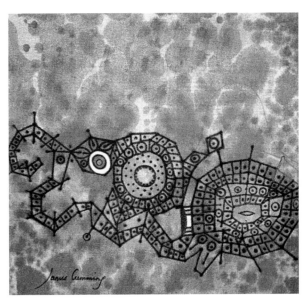

James Cumming 'Gemete'.
oil.

and students of Edinburgh College of Art. Cumming's neo-romantic work with a tartan brogue travelled well, his taut, attenuated monumental figures - as much in the vein of Keith Vaughan as of Robert Colquhoun - later giving away to a Miro-like all-over biomorphic abstraction featuring flowing amoebic creatures in a fluid, atmospheric or sub-aquatic environment. The marked dichotomy between early and recent styles prompted Gerald Smith to note that in the later category "subject matter is no longer the normally visible world but the secret world revealed by the electron microscope".[5] Concerns about the marketability of these Tanguyesque surreal works were allayed when the exhibition sold out. "The relationship with Marjorie Parr became one of friendship and happiness" it was later reported.

Parr's interest in abstract sculpture extended beyond the anthropomorphism of the Hepworth-influenced St Ives 'school' to embrace metropolitan 'New Generation' styles informed by new industrial processes and technological materials. Mark Ingram's exhibition of geometric sculpture in wide-ranging materials like painted wood, fibreglass and aluminium displayed a correspondingly wide variety of abstract form which was, according to Barbara Wright, "very well arranged"[6] in several rooms and the back garden of the London gallery. Kent-born and Watford-trained Ingram, who exhibited 30 mainly painted wood pieces, including the centerpiece 'Fettaie', brought something of his previous life as painter into proceedings, his chromatic organic shapes in the round sharing something with the decorative gestalt of New Generation sculptors like David Annesley, Phillip King, Michael Bolus and William Tucker then being

Mark Ingram and sculptures in courtyard
Marjorie Parr Gallery, Kings Road, 1969.

Guy Worsdell 'Split Form', 1968.
oil.

promoted by Waddington and Alastair McAlpine. A commercial illustrator who had lived in Cornwall, Ingram began making wood structures in 1961 and enjoyed an Arnolfini exhibition in 1963. Margaret Lovell's sculptures, though eschewing Ingram's pastel colours for the polish and verdigris of hard metal, shared an interest in organic form suggestive of leaves, stems or other thin, subtly inflected plant-like objects. Ingram's June exhibition was followed, during July and August, by a large display of studio pottery, among it work by Janet Leach, William Marshall and Michael Truscott. This was complimented by Guy Wordsell's gestural compositions including 'Split Form' (1968).

By the autumn, with the St Ives gallery up and running, the Kings Road gallery reverted to type, if not hype, and the discrete art of promoting some of its most prized artists through the agency of the solo exhibition. That autumn Marjorie presented an eclectic, historically diverse, range of exhibitions from Thetis Blacker paintings and batik wall hangings accompanied by Catherine Yarrow pots in September, to first a full scale John Milne sculpture show with recent paintings by Breon O'Casey in October, and then a November blockbuster '200 Years of English Watercolours'. Not untypically the year closed with a mixed display of small and therefore saleable sculpture alongside gouaches by the vintage Polish-born French cubist master Henri Hayden (1883-1970) then nearing the end of his long and distinguished career.

Marjorie Parr with Denis Mitchell's 'Thrust'
bronze and John Milne's 'Gnathos' bronze.
Photo: P.E.C. Smith.

The September Blacker exhibition was a first with Marjorie, the Surrey-born and educated Glyndebourne vocalist-turned-artist having met Marjorie through the poet Kathleen Raine and painter Cecil Collins during the mid 1960s. Thetis' mastery of the ancient oriental batik technique - waxing and dying fabrics to create pictures, banners, altar fontals, clerical vestments or other decorative hangings - yielded fabulously-coloured and imaginatively varied images that drew on mythic source material. These included banners at Winchester Cathedral and St George's Chapel, Windsor. After a debut painting exhibition at Bear Lane, Oxford in 1959 Blacker spent the 1960s

Thetis Blacker 'Phoenix'.
Batik wax and procion dye.

developing her chosen craft, inspired first by a 1960 trip to Peru (she had some Peruvian blood through her psychiatrist father) where an interest in indigenous Andean art was formed, then by textile studies at Chelsea School of Art between 1961 and 1964. The 1969 show was therefore both culmination and vindication of long studies on, and mastery of, a demanding medium, Richard Walker commenting that "the only conscious element is superb craftsmanship".[7] Walker also spoke of "aeons of ancestral experience" by which was meant a transcendental "beauty and significance very rare in the self conscious 'self expressionist' occidental contemporary art". Blacker's work was indeed attributed with possessing Jungian archetypal and collective imagery beyond the limits of individual vision. Yarrow's vividly textured pots, which Walker explained were "surfaced like the insides of oyster shells" complemented Blacker's mix of heady and tactile, spiritual and earthy.

While Milne and O'Casey provided a well-matched exhibition of Cornish contemporaries who

John Milne exhibition, Kings Road, October 1969.
Photo: Peter Kinnear.

had been sometime assistants under Hepworth, O'Casey harboured long-term pique at being given what he saw as the subordinate upper floor slot. Both however, received ringing endorsement in their catalogues, the eminent critic-curator Bryan Robertson's Milne essay complemented by a less intellectual, though committed and heartfelt, note on O'Casey from friend and colleague Denis Mitchell. Bearing monosyllabic titles like 'Seascape', 'Sunset' or 'Island', O'Casey's minimal-like paintings contained a mysteriousness of form and colour, prompting Mitchell to observe that they possessed the "power of growing on you and some of his most beautiful paintings, in muted colours, only reveal their great depth and lyrical qualities after a long time of intimate familiarity."

John Milne exhibition extended into courtyard.

The subtle planar shifts of Milne's monolithic sculptures, meanwhile, also exuded an anthropomorphic mystery and enigmatic presence. The patiently crafted, Brancusi-influenced marble 'The Kiss' and 'Easter Island Form' or the cold cast 'Totemic Form' and 'Landscape Form' achieved these qualities either in the interior ground floor gallery or, where 'The Kiss' and 'Easter Island Form' were concerned, in the outer courtyard.

The November watercolour exhibition provided a diverse focus on a quintessential English medium that had always been linked to the native landscape school. Capturing the light, atmosphere and temperate damp climate, watercolour captured a 'genius loci' either in terms of pastoral topography or tinted architectural drawing. From the spiky modernity of Alan Reynolds' early 'Red Hopgarden' (1957) or Patrick Hall's lyrical panoramas through the early modern impressionism of Robert Bevan, the Nash brothers, Lucien Pissarro and Muirhead Bone and finally back to old masters like David Cox (1783-1859), Peter de Wint (1784-1849) and William Turner of Oxford (1789-1862) the exhibition traced the development of a demanding native tradition that linked drawing to full-blown painting.

Chapter Four

'A Knack for Selling' 1970-75

The Marjorie Parr Gallery was transformed at the start of 1970. Remaining closed throughout January for a major revamp the gallery re-opened in early February with the remit that "In 1970 all floors will be used for

Douglas Portway and Michael Black exhibition in modernised gallery, February 1970.
Photo: Peter Kinnear.

Paintings, Sculpture, Prints and Pottery." The glass department was discontinued though due to consumer discontent was reinstated as a minor feature of the Lower gallery. The 1970 look was less an antique shop than a chic modernist art gallery, moving on from Portobello Road retro to the designer minimalism of

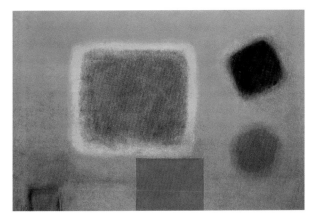

Douglas Portway 'Untitled'.
oil on paper.

more recent Bond Street taste. Too eclectic and diverse to be pinned down to a single aesthetic programme the gallery nonetheless committed itself to progressive or abstract trends in contemporary plastic and applied arts. A joint show of Douglas Portway paintings and Michael Black sculpture launched the new gallery.

Douglas and Caroline Portway.
Photo: Peter Kinnear.

'Untitled' by Portway was reproduced on the cover of 'Arts Review' which featured a full page article by Max Wykes-Joyce on what this prominent critic and abiding gallery friend termed the triumphantly opened, newly furbished gallery.*[1]

Portway's soft edged, low key 'colour field' abstracts were followed, during March, by the very different still life and interior compositions of David Evans. The calm, detached quietism of Evans' almost metaphysical paintings used abstract art's simplified planes of colour to fashion scenarios similar in style and spirit to Magritte, Morandi, early Cockrill, Jeffrey Edwards and Hockney. While fulfilling a conventional taste for neatness and verisimilitude Evans' paintings were neither concretely realist nor, in the words of

David Evans 'The Table', 1969.
oil.

Michael Black and Lady Roll.
Photo: Peter Kinnear.

Peter Eugene Ball 'Birdman'.
copper and brass.

reviewer Richard Walker, an "expression of private ego emotions". Walker instead detected a "feeling of attunement, a condition of empathy between artist and object which is often long in coming to fruition".[*2]

During April the gallery emulated the Portway and Black exhibitions with another joint display between a painter and sculptor. The primitive, folky sculptures of Peter Eugene Ball and 43 Hinterglas paintings by Pauline Kraay were accompanied by John Piper prints. Parr's aversion to prints - which she saw as fragile, low budget commodities with vexed distinctions between original or reproduction status - was wavered where the graphic work of a popular, modern master like Piper was concerned. Between Ball's brass, wood and copper sculptures and Kraay's use of an ancient decorative craft an unusual, ethnic note was sounded, 'Art and Antiques' magazine finding "both of them out-of-line in a fascinating way". It also judged that Marjorie's stable "no longer have the look of being second-hand émigrés from Bond Street and the West End... it becomes steadily more obvious that this gallery is not only bringing big names to Chelsea. Marjorie Parr is finding some interesting new creators". Clearly she was finding her feet and chancing her arm and backing talent she believed in, a situation evident in a substantial catalogue designed to interest potential clients without time to visit the gallery.

The same "out-of-line" creativity characterised Robert Scott Simon's 'clock' sculptures. These accompanied a May exhibition of 40 gesturally assertive, strongly coloured informal abstract paintings (oil, acrylic, gouache or watercolour) by Jeff Hoare. Birmingham-born and Ipswich-trained Scott Simon, a mechanical engineer who worked for W.S. Cowell in Ipswich - the renowned printers who produced the

Robert Scott Simon 'Kinetic Clocks'.

'School Prints' series - and later for Stanley Jones (Scott Simon was managing director of Curwen Prints from 1964-68) made totemic sculptures incorporating working clocks. These struck a surreal-like interplay

35

between form and function. Chelsea-trained Hoare, after a period schoolteaching, taught part-time at the Camberwell and Central schools of art, London and at South Illinois University where participation in Allan Kaprow's landmark 'Happenings' liberated his painting. Indeed the Englishman's informalism utilised free-play mark, chance and accidental colour combinations of an often atmospheric nature.

Hoare's sizeable 1970 exhibition, the first of four with Marjorie, vindicated the dealer's immediate response to an already mature artist who had enjoyed a solo 1964 Piccadilly Gallery exhibition and been an Artist in Residence in Illinois in 1968. Nevertheless Hoare later explained the importance of Parr at a crucial stage stating that "she gave me such encouragement backing my every new direction... without her support I would not have the confidence to progress".*3 Hoare's direct approach to the gallery at the instigation of Michael Rothenstein during autumn 1969 therefore paid dividends, the dealer complementing the artist's experiments during the early 1970s on large scale murals for Universities in Lancaster and Guildford by creating a market for smaller, domestic pictures for the average home.

Henri Hayden's death during the Hoare exhibition brought an era to an end. Hayden's vital early years as a late cubist in the 'rococco' vein of Gris and Marcoussis led to more conventional still life and landscape phases that remained, however, informed by the structural rigour and 'plastic' colour of the experimental cubist years upon which the Polish-born French artist's reputation is based. Hayden's work, loaned from Waddingtons, gave Parr's clients opportunities to access later work by an established modern master whose continuing popularity was propelled not only through these London dealers but also through the major 1966 exhibition 'Hayden's Cezannesque and Cubist Period' at Roland, Browse and Delbanco and a large retrospective at the Museé d'Art Modern, Paris in 1968.

During summer 1970 Marjorie promoted her sculptors, some of whom featured both in 'Ten Sculptors Two Cathedrals' outside Winchester (July-August) and Salisbury (August-September) cathedrals and in 'Shapes in Spaces' at Woburn Park Garden Centre. Although the latter exhibition, which featured Roger Leigh and John Milne from Marjorie's stable, was arranged by the Oxford Gallery and Annely Juda Fine Art, the Marjorie Parr Gallery pitched in by mounting a contemporaneous show 'Sculpture and Ceramics for Out of Doors'. This used the familiar courtyard at the back. Brian Hornal singled out a west country trio - Milne, Leigh and Thursby - as using the outdoors most imaginatively, Milne's 'Totemic 11' making "a positive virtue of simple form and relatively

Peter Thursby 'Leaning Section'. aluminium.

large scale", and Leigh's site specific work "powerful enough to exist in the face of nature's competition." The latter's architecture and planning background naturally inclined his work towards an environmental context, one in which, Hornal argued, "form (as scale modulation) must dominate any obvious content".*4 Margaret Lovell, who shortly before had a solo June exhibition, also tackled this challenge well even if other gallery sculptors were inherently domestic. The domestic intimacy of the gallery reclaimed its place during the autumn which saw Kate Nicholson paintings exhibited alongside Jupp Dernbach-Mayen sculpture during September, an exhibition of various potters including Hans Coper and Lucie Rie displayed alongside Patrick Hall watercolours during October and another John Hitchens recent paintings show in November.

A commercially expedient run-of-the-mill Christmas exhibition, which enjoyed a crowded opening party, proved "an extremely pleasant" mix for the critic Marina Vaizey. The perceived eclecticism of abstract sculptors Anthony Twentyman and Margaret Lovell, kineticist Nigel Van Wieck, studio potter Ewen Henderson, batik artist Thetis Blacker, abstract painters Douglas Portway and Jeff Hoare and so-called naif painter John Christopherson "displays the strength of the gallery". Vaizey's estimation of a show "much suited to domestic interiors" contrasted with Parr's involvement with the outdoor nature of larger sculpture earlier that year. The display did though include some photographs of outdoor installations by gallery sculptors, a theme pertinent to 1970 in terms of the outdoor sculpture at Winchester and Salisbury and of course in her own courtyard.

An artist who shone out from the Christmas show Nigel Van Wieck, provided the opening exhibition in 1971, the exhibition 'Kinetics-Perspex + Light' running throughout January. Van Wieck's perspex rods grouped in simple geometric formations to create intricate relationships between modular parts and the whole belonged to the late constructivist Kinetic movement. Reviewer James Heard's regret over Van Wieck's omission from the major Hayward Gallery Kinetic Art survey the previous year was only partly mitigated by Van Wieck's large solo exhibition at the Graves Art Gallery, Sheffield (Jan) and at Plymouth City Art Gallery (May). A fifty-work James Cumming exhibition in February comprised a combination of hard-edge and Miroesque whimsy.

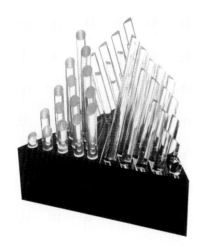

In terms of a March exhibition of over 30 recent sculptures, many uneditioned bronzes, by Salisbury-born but Exeter-based Peter Thursby, the gallery moved from the kinetics of Van Wieck to a static late modernist idiom based on the abstract monolith. The pronounced architectural or mechanical element in

Betty Holman 'The Salvation Army', 1970.
oil.

sculptures like 'Mo-Xylophonic Section' saw Thursby's sculpture move away from St Ives anthropomorphism to evoke more urban Paolozzi-like themes. Shared with Betty Holman whose paintings like 'The Salvation Army' and a group of Spanish and St Ives subjects were described by reviewer Marina Vaizey as "flat, naive, cheerful and charming... little confections for our lighter moments",*5 the Thursby exhibition was the culmination of a long, steady 'courtship' between artist and dealer. Despite taking their inspiration from industrial, mechanical or architectural sources massive forms like 'Single Tower', 'Double Wall' and 'Divided Block' conjured for Vaizey "some sort of secular temple, a Stonehenge for the twentieth century", the interface between ancient and modern, sharing with Moore, Dalwood, Turnbull and Paolozzi a re-interpretation of primitive ritual adapted to modern function.

Bernard Leach with Janet Leach and Lucie Rie.
Photo: Peter Kinnear.

Bernard Leach Pots.
stoneware and porcelain.

During April a joint display of Bernard Leach's pots and calligraphic paintings in Japanese inks by Donatienne Sapriel exchanged the unlikely, even discordent, Thursby/Holman pairing for a genuine artistic osmosis, Caroline Shaw in 'The Connoisseur' describing the ink drawings as having "sympathetic Eastern affinities" which shared with Leach "qualities of simplicity and conviction". Cottie Burland in 'Arts Review' similarly sensed the overlap between Sapriel's ink paintings of fruits and birds which carried the iconic, symbolic and decorative power of glazed ceramic décor, and Leach's anglo-oriental pots where "Decorative is kept at a level of utmost simplicity".*6 This was followed by a prints and drawings show in keeping with the lightness of early summer. Marjorie was not, as we have seen, normally given to graphics though a glut of the prolific John Piper lithographs, Canterbury Tales etchings by Elisabeth Frink, etchings by Ben Nicholson and a set of Barbara Hepworth lithographs (the Aegean Suite) provided appealing items by big name artists.

In June a solo exhibition of 36 recent paintings, mainly oil and cryla on board, by the Scottish-born St Ives artist W. Barns-Graham registered the influence on 'head office' of the St Ives 'branch'. Given that many 'local' St Ives artists like Roy Conn or Bob Crossley never graduated from the group show at

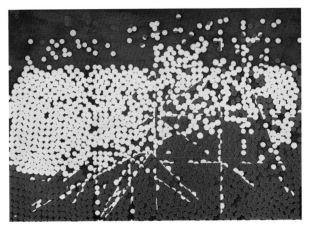

W. Barns-Graham.
oil and cryla on board.

Will's Lane, Barns-Graham's solo in the capital reflected both personal artistic ambition and the kudos that Marjorie's gallery now enjoyed. While pictures like 'Blue Discs on Black' or 'Vermilion and White Discs on Bright Red' (1971) deployed titles based on salient colour arrangements, a situation concomittent with the plasticity and abstraction of Barns-Graham's work, the exhibition represented for Richard Walker "an algebraic equation for human life". A redolent Scottishness also translated itself, Walker observing "an indissoluable marriage of intellect and passion, peculiarly Scottish in the degree to which one is inseparable from the other".[*7] Furthermore the wind and wave themes of both linear and coloured spot compositions reflected a residual naturalism. Barns-Graham's place within the post-war St Ives School was secured through the characteristic use of abstract, even mathematical, composition with oblique, though tangible, landscape associations. Small Giacometti-like stick figures in bronze by Marcia Panama, summarised by Walker as "expressionist evocations of athletic balance, tension, flowing movement" accompanied the Barns-Grahams.

Marcia Panama.
bronze.

The versatility of Marjorie Parr Gallery was such that contemporary prints by well-known modern masters followed by the promotion of a front rank St Ives painter led to the contrasting historical exhibition 'Chelsea in the 19th Century' comprising Whistler, Greaves and Roussel. The vexed artistic issues of the day centred around the aesthetic movement and Whistler's precious art-for art's-sake formalism. What constituted the boundaries of fine art printmaking and

St Ives group exhibition Austin Reed Gallery, London, August 1971.
Photo: Peter Kinnear.

Marjorie Parr opening John Milne's exhibition
City Art Gallery, Plymouth, June 1971.
Photo: Peter Kinnear.

the degree to which academic painting could be reduced to nocturnal reduction and atmospheric silhouette were issues that Whistler argued with Ruskin and Sickert as part of his 'gentle art of making enemies'. Stylistic arguments apart, Chelsea was central both to Whistler's art and that of his followers. Through their virtuoso draughtsmanship, topographic insight and graphic verve with printmaking they created what reviewer Michael Webber termed "insight into the character of the area". The documentary and historical interest in featuring works from an age before Chelsea entered the modern era and changed forever was such that, the following summer, Marjorie presented a sequel, 'Chelsea in the 18th and 19th Centuries'. A third and final St Ives Group exhibition at Austin Reed Gallery, London during August included works from Marjorie Parr.

This high summer extravaganza was followed by an autumn season of solo exhibitions by favoured gallery artists. Thetis Blacker's batik paintings, recent sculpture by Denis Mitchell and Douglas Portway paintings commanded three well-illustrated catalogues, a novelty at the time that saw the documented focus on recent work as a useful promotional tool and commercial strategy. A fully illustrated Blacker catalogue contained a note on the laborious though rewarding process of batik, a biography and artist's statement among which was a warm tribute to the support of Parr, and an anthology of recent press cuttings among them pertinent pieces by Walker and Wykes-Joyce. Marina Vaizey applauded "a handsome presence, lively manner, enthusiasm and sparkling intelligence, dedication and warmth", personal attributes that shone through in the work, the "fiendishly difficult methods" of batik notwithstanding. Both Vaizey in 'Arts Review' and Terence Mullaly in the 'Daily Telegraph' spoke of the artist's colour, the former alluding to its

Thetis Blacker 'Garuda' cover design for Blacker
exhibition, September 1971.

Denis Mitchell 'Tolver', 1971.
lime wood.

"unique depth" the latter to the fact that "colour is not so much vivid as glowing with inner fires". The artist's recent visit to the Batik Research Institute, Java, courtesy of a Churchill Fellowship, was reflected in the sumptous dyed colours onto unsealed white cotton.

Denis Mitchell, like Blacker, enjoyed a warm rapport with Parr, acknowledging a debt of gratitude when writing "You made so much possible for me and granted my greatest wish to live on my work." But unlike Blacker's, Mitchell's catalogue was black and white - colour being dispensible for sculpture - and contained an essay by his friend and colleague, the collector and painter George Dannatt. 'Probus' on the front and 'Tolver' (1971) on the back cover adhered to a predilection for slimness and uprightness. Other 1971 pieces like 'St Merryn', 'Endellion' and 'St Kevern' stood like mysterious sentinels, a feeling of watchfullness enhanced by slits or the vigilant symmetry of eye-like cavities.

Mitchell's use of Cornish titles was temporarily jettisoned in 1971. The slim needle-like 'Cerrito', extended bronze 'Cordoba' and 'Cauca' (1971) for example, used South American titles that reflected a 1970 lecture tour of Columbia where he taught for a month at the University of the Andes in Bogota. Despite this Richard Walker detected "intimations of archaic influence, particularly Minoan Crete" and "a counterpoint of form and force, form and space" in symmetrically designed monolithic bronze sculptures

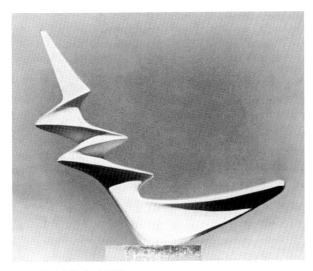

Denis Mitchell 'Probus', 1971
bronze

carrying lyrical interplay between open and closed, polished and patinated surfaces. A decade after leaving her workshop Mitchell had created an independent identity from Barbara Hepworth, Walker triggering the gender argument that "his

41

work is forceful, masculine where hers is womblike, contained".

The November Douglas Portway exhibition which followed Denis Mitchell was the South Africa-born painter's first solo in London since 1968 forays with the Travers and Drian galleries. Portway's large, often abstract, paintings combined geometry with informalism, hard edge and randomly-applied amorphous areas of colour. Through his seamless integration of discipline and abandon Portway revealed an intimate induction into modern painting to which he was introduced through magazine reproductions and then a formative scholarship to New York in 1952. Here the influence of Zen ideas and of emerging 'abstract expressionist' painting enabled him, in Richard Walker's words, "to transcend provincial beginnings, to discover himself".[8] The example of William Scott and Alan Davie notwithstanding, Portway's unusually early exposure to the New York School anticipated its absorption by a British audience later in the decade. Portway's preference for abstraction was not, in Walker's eyes, "for didactic reasons" but rather contained the possibilities of rich cosmologic or architectural metaphor even within the confines of a broadly non-representational language.

Douglas Portway 'Oracle III', 1971.
oil on canvas.

Walker's summation of "the basic Portway of fine texture, dusky secretive colour, sensitively primitive line" described a by now mature artist in mid career. A solo Jesse Watkins exhibition in January 1972 comprised 20 sculptures, mainly in steel (there were 5 bronzes), from an experienced sculptor who had previously exhibited with the Drian Gallery. The Goldsmiths and Chelsea trained artist turned from painting and industrial design to sculpture in the late 1950s, subsequently pursuing a metier that

Jesse Watkins 'Pisces'.
steel.

Anthony Caro made popular during the 1960s at St Martins School of Art, London. The catalogue cover featured the mobile 'Pisces', that stated both Watkins' engineering nous and outdoor sensibility. Like the indoor sculptures 'Pisces' represented a metaphorical minimalism or, as reviewer Gerald Smith put it, "a joyful warmth" beyond the "hard edges and polished surfaces". The abstract painter Denis Bowen, whose interview with Watkins accompanied Smith's review, did, however, take a formalist line remarking that Watkins had "eliminated all the spikes and excrescences and become very pure and hard edged".[9] Bowen shared with Watkins a Royal Navy background (Watkins was a commander during the War) and a professional association with Macedonia, where both artists were given civic recognition.

A February Peter Ball exhibition 'Primitive Sculpture' was described by Marina Vaizey as containing "beautifully constructed and impeccably crafted images".[10] This was particularly true of the totemic 'Harpy and the Poet' in wood, copper and brass. Ball's primitivism was transformed into a contemporary context, the ethnic, ritualistic or folky content "never mere pastiche" according to Vaizey. The juxtaposition of Watkins and Ball exhibitions highlighted the gallery's eclectic diversity, a contemporaneous exhibition 'Artists from Marjorie Parr' at Austin Reed in Regent Street providing curatorial definition of the essential Marjorie Parr taste in terms of Oswell Blakeston's description of a show "most rewarding for art lovers who seek nourishment rather than debate". This salient comment alluded to a worthwhile aesthetic mainstream, rather than cutting

Peter Eugene Ball 'Harpy and the Poet'.
wood, copper and brass.

Jeff Hoare 'New Hampshire', 1972.
acrylic.

edge corner, the gallery providing a palatable stable for middle-of-the-road taste. Among this was the salubrious colourism of Hoare and Blacker and life-affirming abstracted forms of Mitchell, Milne, Lovell and Watkins.

Jeff Hoare paintings during March provided promise of light and colour at winter's end. The liquid nature of paint as a mercurial substance governed the gestural tempo and momentary magic of Hoare's work for which the medium of watercolour provided the truest vehicle. Gloucestershire watercolours by Hoare used "deeper, more intense colours" according to Richard Smart who detected the inherent quality of watercolour even in acrylics based on the New Hampshire landscape.

During the course of 1972 Marjorie's efforts with sculpture, after the initial displays of Watkins and Ball early that year, concentrated on John Milne and Margaret Lovell both of whom enjoyed significant solo exhibitions on the Kings Road in April and September respectively. This crucial period in their careers was overseen by Parr who also played an important role in their respective retrospectives at Plymouth City Art Gallery in June 1971 and June 1972. Indeed A.A. Cumming, the Plymouth curator, provided the catalogue note for Milne's Parr exhibition writing that "like Hepworth and Moore his roots were in the north but the Cornish environment, the habitat of his adoption, has left a clear mark". Nevertheless, among the 36 mainly recent sculptures and 10 reliefs in various materials ranging from wood (guarea and mahogony) to cold cast aluminium, bronze and

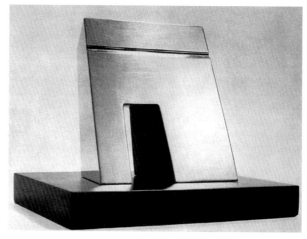

John Milne 'Cyrus', 1972.
bronze.
Photo: P.E.C. Smith.

stainless steel were free-standing forms like 'Darius', 'Landscape Isfahan', 'Persian Monolith' and 'Cyrus' that reflected Milne's passion for north African or

*Margaret Lovell 'Barquentine III'.
bronze.*

Middle-Eastern landscapes and Islamic architecture. The artist indeed spoke of a "sense of mystery and intense awe" inspired by recent Persian travels.

The small polished bronze 'Cyrus', illustrated in Duncan James' review which declared a preponderance of "lyrical rather than aggressive, static rather than dynamic" shapes, belonged to a group of generally small scale works inspired by Persian themes. Such interests had, Milne wrote, exerted "as great an impact upon my work as those early visits to Greece and Morocco". Whatever the, cultural or religious source Milne's sculpture had, according to eminent critic and editor Bernard Denvir, achieved "an allusive quality" countering the generic "insularity" of Cornish art. What Denvir also saw as a "plastic austerity... beyond the romantic naturalism"*[11] of later Hepworth reflected a much-travelled Milne's exposure not only to the favoured exotic locations but also to the endemic contemporary influence of minimalism. Nevertheless Hepworth, as neighbour, mentor and one-time employer, remained an important presence in Milne's life and visited the Parr exhibition with her secretary Brian Smith that April and continued to give genuine, if guarded, encouragement to the younger sculptor.

Margaret Lovell's solo September exhibition followed her large 75-work sculpture retrospective in Plymouth in June. Like the Milne exhibition six months earlier Lovell's comprised sculptures in diverse materials (bronze, marble, alabaster, slate and polyphant stone) and used A.A. Cumming as critical champion in the catalogue. This publication, with the upright, leaf-like bronze form 'Barquentine III' on the cover, was a near replica of the Plymouth catalogue with inside adjustments to the exhibits listing. Given the Slade-trained Bristolian sculptor's roots Cumming wrote that "it is not surprising that the symbols of the sea have captured her attention" though the axiomatically titled 'Barquentine' made allusion to the billowing shapes of sails or windjammers as well as perhaps more frequent distillations of plant or leaf shapes. Indeed, 'Petal' was reproduced as the catalogue frontispiece. Both maritime and organic themes were therefore observed by reviewer Richard Walker who sensed "the dynamics of wind, tall sail and embedding sea captured in the main triangular sail forms" on the one hand and "minimal modification of material which offers suggestion of organic form" on the other*.[12]

Invariably containing a single Magritte-like figure in frozen contemplation of the sterile surrounding scene, David Evans' paintings like 'Ystrad Revisited' from his May 1972 exhibition belonged to what Peter Dyke felt were the three recurring themes of Evans' work, namely the road, tower and bridge. What Dyke

*David Evans 'Ystrad Revisited'.
oil.*

called the "lonely invasion of the privacy of the still countryside"*13 by these iconic, man-made landmarks contained implicit philosophic content concerning man's relationship to the natural world. Furthermore the characteristic use of cool, detached imagery, courtesy of hard edge abstraction, photo realism and late surrealist metaphysics, were stylistically pertinent and entirely of the late modernist moment.

Walter Greaves 'Chelsea Old Church and Archway'.

The mid-summer exhibition 'Chelsea and Kensington in the 18th and 19th centuries', which conspired with 'The Wonderful Village' at the Michael Parkin Gallery to focus on the local artistic heritage of Chelsea, took Marjorie Parr away from pre-occupations with the promotion of younger or contemporary artists. The inevitable and continuing spell of Whistler was a feature of both exhibitions and so too was the work of his followers Walter Greaves and Mortimer Mempes, the latter represented with several etched portrait studies of the master. Parkin's previous exhibition in May had in fact focussed on Whistler's four closest artistic disciples. Francis Watson dedicated a full page review of both Parr and Parkin shows in the 'Arts Review'.

During July the gallery witnessed a return to contemporary themes and a business-as-usual show which did, however, introduce two artists - Bryan Illsley

Janet and Bernard Leach with Bryan Illsley's painting of pots, July 1972. Photo: Harley Carpenter.

and Tony O'Malley - who previously had been somewhat anonymously displayed in mixed exhibitions at the St Ives gallery. Pots by Janet Leach were also included and used simple but strong and elemental forms; these neither lost touch with traditional function nor entered the sculptural ceramic arena. The Texan-born St Ives-based potter's unaffected forms were uncompromisingly earthy and, in Richard Walker's eyes, possessed "a rugged strength... sparsely and naturally decorated"*14 for which Bernard Leach's third wife used traditional Japanese techniques such as

Bernard and Janet Leach in the 'Bistingo' restaurant with Guy Worsdell, Mary Lambert and Pat Gelley.

'raku' and fortuitous wood-fired glazing effects. Bryan Illsley, whose brother Leslie helped start the popular Troika Pottery in St Ives, once worked in the Leach Pottery; his Braque-like still life subjects which Walker felt "blend aptly" with the Leach pots in the ground floor gallery, changed into brighter colours upstairs where Illsley's paintings "add a note of gaity to contrast the geologic monumentality" of O'Malley.

The Celtic quality of O'Malley's work reminded us of a key aspect of St Ives art after the Marjorie Parr Gallery's Cornish branch had been sold. Its distinctively physical style contrasted with the more urban styles of the August mixed exhibition in which the cerebral, patterned Miroesque abstraction of James Cumming, the "more static, monumental" compositions of Douglas Portway's suave, sophisticated 'field' paintings and Plazzotta's neo-classical figurative sculptures dominated. But Vivien ap Rhys Pryce's tiny bronzes of 'controposto' dancing figures and the debutante Tommy Rowe's steel constructions, described by Walker as "playful, strong, and aero-dynamically convincing",[15] made

Marjorie Parr Gallery, October 1972.

47

*John Hitchens 'High Mountain Dusk'.
oil.*

worthwhile additions to a summer season show by gallery artists. By virtue of being a trusted technical assistant to Hepworth, Milne and Mitchell, Rowe was a newcomer in name only and offered something different and unique with his welded pieces.

John Hitchens' October 1972 show with the regulation three dozen pictures was his seventh solo with Parr. Richard Smart's estimation that "only a clever painter could leave so much unstated"[*16] indicated the successful integration of abstraction with the mercurial subject of changing weather and elements in flux. Such content indeed represented a point of departure - literally so - from place-specific topography, 'Moorland Cloud', 'High Mountain Dusk' and a series of 'Woodland Water' compositions encapsulating, all the same, the verdant pastoral landscape of the English 'school' at large. From the romantic naturalism

Nigel Van Wieck working in his studio.

of Hitchens to the cerebral geometry in high tech materials of Nigel Van Wieck's November 1972 exhibition 'Perspex-Light + Sound' put on by Marjorie at Austin Reed, the gallery remained a broad stylistic church. Patrick Hall's December exhibition, which shared Hitchens' breezy gesturalism, was described by reviewer Michael Shepherd as "beautifully

Patrick and Mary Hall, 1970.
Photo: Peter Kinnear.

composed, taken aptly from nature, but filtered and refined into a song of the unpolluted landscape of the heart".*17 But Hall alighted on specific places, prompting Shepherd to observe that "where Dufy is master of the breeze and flutter of the port, Patrick Hall is master of the golden, sandy beach at low tide, the sea pool and the estuary, often of the same Normandy and Brittany". 'Beach Normandy', illustrated on the exhibition card, emulated the exhilarating plein air impressionism of the north coast, Hall's genius for atmospheric stain and smudge, for diaphanous, transparent light and for the tinted topographic sweep in full evidence.

Not for the first time Marjorie Parr began 1973 - her penultimate one in full charge of the gallery - with a timely exhibition dovetailed with a corresponding one in another gallery. As with the shared Chelsea show in 1972 Marjorie's exhibition 'Primitive Paintings' was featured alongside the Archer Gallery's 'Fantastic and Naive Reality' in 'Arts Review'. Richard Shone's description, that the exhibition "has the inevitable St Ives flavour but some European painters are included",*18 characterised Marjorie's project at large,

Patrick Hall 'Beach Normandy', 1972.
watercolour.

her commitment to St Ives modernism complemented by a historical focus on modern masters from the Ecole de Paris or other significant schools. The naive and primitive was a distinct strand within the St Ives 'school', the legacy of Alfred Wallis, Christopher Wood, Mary Jewels and others informing, among others, the latter-day primitivism of Bryan Pearce, Bob Bourne, Joan Gillchrest, Fred Yates, Linda Weir and Simeon Stafford. Indeed Betty Holman was seen by Shone as "of the Wallis/Lowry stamp... lots of stiff figures against Cornish harbours". Gillian Beckles, Kenneth Hayes, Moshe Maurer and Peter Ball offered eclectic variety. The latter's pieces like 'King, Queen and Fool' and 'Mermaid', in "marrying Africana with 17th century church monuments" struck an analogy with Bernard Leach's eclectic compound of oriental and indiginous English slipware strands.

The John Piper exhibition 'Recent Paintings, Graphics, Pottery' which followed in February 1973 was recycled from the West End (Marlborough Fine Art), prompting Karen Usborne to write: "That the work of such a prominent artist can be seen at a less prominent gallery is a credit to the enterprise of Marjorie Parr".[19] Piper's multi-facetted and experimental project saw paintings - like the large picture 'Brittany Beach' illustrated on the exhibition card - decorated pottery, drawings, screenprints and photography, the latter concentrating on what for the topographic Piper was the new subject of women. This new departure prompted Usborne to report, perhaps over-generously, on "quite the most exciting" work Piper had yet done. Piper attended the Private View.

John Piper 'Brittany Beach'.
oil.

Another major artist, the eminent and much-loved painter Anne Redpath, doyen of the Edinburgh 'school' and first woman painter member of the Royal Scottish Academy, filled the March slot. The exhibition card featured 'Houses and Hens, Corsica' in colour, a subject that displayed Redpath's uncanny Scottish alliance of topographic cragginess, textural grittiness, formal robustness and chromatic lyricism. It also revealed her Scottish relish for travel, particularly to France (where she was domiciled for part of the inter-war period) and the Mediterranean. Terence Mullaly spoke of Redpath's "remarkably wide range of colour, brushwork of freedom and strength",[20] qualities that reflected the free and seamless inter-changeability of art and life. Indeed, two of Redpath's three sons, the Edinburgh lecturer David Michie and Dorset-based

Anne Redpath 'Houses and Hens, Corsica'. oil.

Alastair, eptomised the natural assimilation of art by also pursuing, albeit less successfully, careers as painters. Michael Shepherd's estimation that Redpath's work "breathes the inimitable air of that painterly Golden Age before the war, when foreign travel was very heaven and Europe was very old, very beautiful and life was care-free... a simple matter of enjoying painting and painting enjoyment"[*21] encapsulated these virtues while integrating the Scottish work ethic with the pleasure principle.

The April exhibition 'John Christopherson', accompanied by Bernard Leach pots, celebrated the work of a painter of very different, more melancholic, persuasion. Christopherson's were tightly designed, obsessively built-up whereas Redpath's were free and painterly. Thematically too, they diverged, the Greenwich-based painter of empty Hampstead and Greenwich streets frozen in time or of densely textured anthropomorphic pictographs contrasting with Redpath's sumptuous church interiors, sensuous still lifes and alternatively sombre or bright quaysides. Christopherson's declared interest in the "ambiguity between ancient and modern" and in the "forlorn poetry of the disregarded" was reflected in his passion for art collecting where the acquisition of works by Paolozzi, Gwyther Irwin, Prunella Clough, early Alan Reynolds and other texturally explicit or romantic artists revealed the peculiarity of Christopherson's interests.

The painting illustrated on the card 'The Red Door' was characteristic of recent work that 'International Herald Tribune' reviewer Max Wykes-Joyce described as "Klee-like, slightly fantastic small figurations of the buildings and streets of Greenwich... unhurried and personal... undeterred by changes in public taste and fashion".[*22] Wykes-Joyce's intimacy with Christopherson's work hit several nerves, his reference to "unhurried and personal" qualities adeptly summarising the self-taught and idiosyncratic artist's preference for what his eventual dealer, Jane England, later described as "slowly and obsessively" worked paintings built up with glazes over weeks, months and even years.

The architectural frontality and symmetry of 'The Red Door' was a generic feature of Christopherson's recent post-1970 works, among them 'Antique Shop (Homage to Balthus)' (1970), 'House in Shooters Hill Road' (1971), 'Entrance to Holly Mount', 'Building at Rye' (1972) and 'Cafe in Kentish Town' (1973). The exhibition card's statement that "although his painting has gradually become more figurative he is still very interested in texture and paint quality" reflected the recurring incidence of graffiti within the pictures, graffiti of either an ethnocentric or, as in these instances, of an inscrutable and alienated kind. Slogans like 'Bob', 'Nowhere', 'Lost' or 'Do Not

John Christopherson 'The Red Door'. oil.

51

Obstruct' functioned as markers of the artist's depressive temperament and feeling of displacement within a modern, if familiar, environment.

Christopherson's apparent imperviousness to "changes in public taste and fashion", while reflecting the lack of an art school background, was belied by his regular presence on the West End gallery and auction room circuit. Both through weekly Bond Street sorties and annual trips to St Ives Christopherson was au fait with art world developments though his own aesthetic allegiance to retrospective 1950s modes like matter painting on the one hand or magic realism on the other set him apart from strictly contemporary trends. Launched through three solo shows with the Leicester Galleries during the later 1960s Christopherson's work was subsequently promoted by Parr who, in providing two London solos in 1973 and 1974 and regular group showings in St Ives, moved his reputation forward from the tentative early to more established later exhibiting career with England & Co. during the 1990s.

By way of complete contrast to Christopherson's vision of the antique, disregarded or melancholic a James Cumming exhibition in May was followed by the florid freshness of South Shields-born and Royal Academy-trained Tom Davison's exhibition of recent flower paintings which the publicity card described as

Tom Davison 'Day Lily'.
oil.

"bold in concept yet intimate in detail and execution". By dint of their large scale these floral subjects were certainly bold, the O'Keeffe-like 'Day Lily' - whose amplified yellow and red petals on an Indian Red background posited an almost abstract foray into pure colour and form - representing the kind of picture on display that Richard Walker felt was "unfittable into the usual botanical illustration or still life categories".*23 The same writer's description of "rich, luminous and vivid" colour did, however, do justice to the pure chromatic intensity of the floral world from which, of course, derived many artist paint pigments. Another reviewer, the Duchess of St Albans, referred to "ultra sophisticated paintings... when rendered on a large scale form unfamiliar motifs".*24

The July exhibition focussed on the work of a sculptor, Lithuanian-born and Canadian-trained Elena Gaputyte (1927-1992), and a renowned potter, Ewen Henderson. Gaputyte was in many ways a figure after Marjorie's heart having run a St Ives gallery, the moderately successful Sail Loft Gallery, from 1960 to 1963, as well as producing strongly delineated a la mode landscape drawings with taut charcoal lines and sculpture that, as the artist explained, amounted to a "realisation of my childhood fantasies and longings".*25 While a harbinger of Marjorie's St Ives gallery starting six years later, the Sail Loft was more akin to an artist's co-operative than a strict down-the-line business, acting as much as social rendezvous as shop. Gaputyte later summarised St Ives as "like a big family, a special type of community which functioned beautifully without planning. People dropped in almost at all times; to argue, to rest, to eat, even to sing".*26 She did not however mention to buy!

Gaputyte's Cornish charcoal drawings which, according to the contemporaneous Newlyn Art Gallery director and abstract painter Michael Canney, possessed "an admirable tautness" and were "painful in their intensity" were superseded by bronze sculptures after her move to London in 1964 and subsequent studies in bronze casting at Hammersmith School of Art. Her interest in archaic precedents and, closer to the time and place of her own origins, in the oeuvre of Constantin Brancusi, the Paris-based Romanian folk carver, was reflected in schematised or pyramid-like bronze figures that sacrificed classical naturalism for archtypal symbolism. While Roy Miles described them as "monuments to the artist's own stateless-ness" the bronzes were, in the final analysis, deemed "not really strong enough to transcend the strong emotions she undoubtedly feels".*27 Miles in fact responded more positively to the "stunningly beautiful artefacts" of Ewen Henderson, finding that the pots "suggest the dried, decaying nature of the earth, leaf and mould". These earthy, organic features associated themselves, through the bulb and fanned

Ewen Henderson 'Two Bottle Forms', c1960. stoneware.
Photo: Anthony Shaw.

Evelyn Williams 'Golden Girl'.
papier mache.

shapes with the intrinsic plasticity and manufacturing processes peculiar to ceramics.

Sculpture of a very different kind followed with the August exhibition 'Reliefs and Wax Sculpture' by St Martins and RCA trained Evelyn Williams (b.1929), an artist whose 100-strong retrospective of work from 1945 to 1972 at the Whitechapel Art Gallery the previous November inspired Marjorie to offer the artist a show. The "domestic and erotic harmony"[*28] of these papier mache dolls with straw hair found an ideal setting in what Brian Wallworth described as the "intimate atmosphere" of Marjorie's gallery, a homely environment contrasting with the institutional uniformity of the Whitechapel. Williams' quest for physical palpability and for breaking the barrier between the spectator and pictorial protagonists took in first impasto and then three dimensional collage and papier maché, a medium stretching back to 1961 when the artist's early sculpture of two heads won a prize in the sculpture section of the John Moores Liverpool competition.

The impetus of this significant early success led to a productive and consistent subsequent career, solo exhibitions after the one with Marjorie following at Riverside Studios, Hammersmith and Graves Art Gallery, Sheffield (1984), Manchester City Art Gallery (1997) and Agnews, London (2003). These reflected a consistency of purpose, the Agnews catalogue essayist Nicholas Usherwood noting how, as at John Moores, the spectator was "forced to abandon his passive role as a mere observer... and take the place of the absent figure... implicated in the picture's concerns".

Amsterdam-born Aart van Kruiselbergen's (b.1936) exhibition of flatly painted architectural or landscape subjects in September was shared with another, equally historically contrasting, exhibition made up of Jessica Dismorr's 1920s paintings of southern France. Both shows employed southern French themes, however, van Kruiselbergen having recently moved to France after spells living in London between the late 1950s and late 1960s (he studied at Sir John Cass School of Art) and then in Portugal during the late 1960s. Like David Evans, Kruiselbergen's work, with a faint touch of surreal stillness and metaphysical mystery, introduced into figuration the flat, hard edged, chromatically assertive style of contemporary post painterly abstraction, a harbinger, perhaps, of post-modern eclecticism, stylistic inclusiveness and pluralism. Both Max Wykes-Joyce and Timothy Mason divined "pure" qualities, the former critic estimating that the "pure" and "austere" pictures "continue the strain originated by Leger and Purists of Paris",[*29] the latter describing "cool and elegant" paintings deemed "simple to the point of plainness".[*30]

Aart van Kruiselbergen 'The Bus'.
oil.
Photo: Rodney Todd-White.

Jessica Dismorr 'Old Street, Cannes', 1925.
watercolour.

Jessica Dismorr's similarly colourful, cosmopolitan career began with studies in France under Metzinger, Segonzac and J.D. Ferguson and continued with notable contributions first to the Salon D'Automne in 1913 then to the London Group and 7&5 Society during the 1920s. Dismorr's historically significant involvement with the Vorticist Manifesto (1915) and contribution to the anti-war publication BLAST yielded portraits in the angular Vorticist style. In watercolours like 'Old Street, Cannes' or in the later portraits of the early 1930s, however, Dismorr's work, which Mason described as "mellow in colour and mood", softened.

In place of a postponed Blacker exhibition a group show of work by sculptors Frink, Chadwick, Hepworth and Moore and by the painters Ivon Hitchens, Nicholson, Pasmore, Piper, Redpath and Sutherland offered a veritable cornucopia of major British moderns at a short remove from these distinguished artist's usual West End exhibition venues. Oils by Douglas Portway continued throughout November 1973. A crisp symmetry characterised the axiomatic 'Still Centre 2', reproduced on the exhibition card, and 'Four White Screens' (1973) an elegant canvas that the collector Dick Allen purchased off Marjorie.

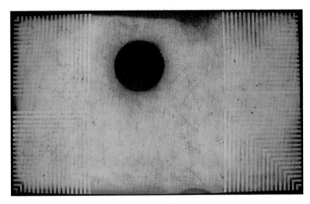

Douglas Portway 'Four White Screens', 1973.
oil.
Photo: Charles Allen.

The recent group of Portways was followed by a Phyllis Mackenzie display, 'The Legal Scene', comprising cartoonish drawings on the theme of courtrooms in session. While Mackenzie was never allowed to work directly in court an acute visual memory and the long arm of her natural graphic wit ensured telling caricatures of both the bright and dark side of life. This was relayed with dashing highlights of red and white on beige paper grounds. Barbara Wright wrote that "the spirit is not so far from Daumier, though never cruel, while always pertinent and clear sighted".[31] The Chelsea Post wrote that the 56-work exhibition's success "lies in the wonderfull expressions" of the protagonists.

The gallery began 1974 - and the final six months with Marjorie in sole command - with an assorted display including Kenneth Hayes, Tom Davison, Pat Douthwaite and Patricia Kahn; the latter's streamlined abstractions like 'The Loving Couple', in Parian marble, recalled Milne's interpretation of Brancusi. The more familiar neo-classical figurative sculpture of Plazzotta followed in February. The Italian-born virtuoso modeller's recurrent preoccupation with the theme of dance yielded the standing yet reposefull duet of 'Symphonic Variations 11' (illustrated on the publicity card) on the one hand and the fully animated 'Swan Lake' on the other, the sculptural interpretation of operatic dance in full flow advertised full page in 'Arts Review'. Richard Smart's accompanying review touched on the problem of movement in the plastic arts, for which Plazzotta's reverberating answer was a Rodin-inspired romantic naturalism trading in the literal depiction of animated musculature, stretched pose and instant exertion. Smart estimated that for an artist whose "fascination is with energy" and who "breathes not just life,but a philosophy of freedom, into his works"[*32] dance was an apt, indeed indispensable, subject possessed of rich iconographic precedence and art historical pedigree.

Phyllis Mackenzie 'Legal Argument 1'.
mixed media.

Marjorie's penchant for new departures made her something of a magpie among London gallerists; an exhibition in March 'Australian Realist Paintings' by Melbourne-born Noel Counihan did, however, chime in its cartoonish way with the Phyllis Mackenzie show, Counihan having worked as a cartoonist and satirical illustrator for both Australian and, during the early 1950s, British newspapers like the 'Daily Mail', as well as for the 'Radio Times'. This left-wing social realist had, the previous year, enjoyed two significant solo exhibitions - at the National Gallery, Victoria and at the Commonwealth Institute, Kensington - the latter featuring over 50 paintings and drawings and 11 prints mostly linocut. Barbara Wright felt "There is surely nothing specifically Australian about him".[*33] This was evidenced by "a profound understanding of, and compassion for, mankind" that was generic rather than Nolanesque or specifically Australian in kind.

The diversity of the gallery's contemporary programme was reflected in the altogether different Jeff Hoare show that followed in April. Chelsea-trained Hoare tapped into that mid Atlantic quintesentialism that appropriated the unfettered freedom ot expression of informal abstract painting. Indeed Hoare's connections with post-war American, particulary New York, painting was significant. He became visiting professor at South Illinois University, where he had a show in 1968, and met Paul Jenkins and Wilhelm de Kooning not long afterwards. Later confessing to being "overwhelmed" by the American art scene and "surprised how open it all was"*34 the English artist later adapted the habits of ambitious avant garde American painting - notably its large scale and public-mindedness - to his later career back in the old world.

These developments were specifically translated into large scale mural paintings produced in situ at Lancaster University (where he was Granada Fellow for two years) and at the University of Surrey, Guildford, where a 60-foot long mural dominated by blues and yellows used the poured paint techniques of Jenkins, and before Jenkins, of Pollock, Frankenthaler, Olitski et al. Hoare also experimented with contrasting paint media, ranging from petrol used to liquify the oil in the murals to seawater in a series of sea paintings. The Marjorie Parr exhibition anticipated shows with Selley Fausset (a fellow lecturer at the Central School who failed in a bid to exhibit with Parr) and Dante Elsner at the South London Gallery, Camberwell the following month and, more auspiciously, with the legendary Bertha Schaeffer, New York in 1975. The Parr show elicited critical ambivalence from Peter Pope who

Jeff Hoare 'Orion', 1973.
oil.

picked up on the problem of naturalistic content within informalism, residual links with the landscape sublime evident in 'Orion', illustrated on the card, and 'Afterglow', a picture "with its idea of a land mass brooding over the dying light of the sun".*35

The month of May provided surrealist tendencies, a Peter Ball sculpture display on the ground floor complemented by the avowedly surrealist art of John Banting. Ball's "Demeter", a hieratic totemic figure constructed with diverse 'found' materials like driftwood, rope and pewter, proved compatible with Banting's surrealism. Surrealism's use of non-academic influences to break down social and aesthetic convention and liberate the spirit certainly extended beyond the party line, pace Breton, to affect non-affiliated artists like Ball whom Oswell Blakeston described as liking "non-official art, such as psychotic art which has a dimension of power".*36 The Englishness of Ball's work, described by Blakeston as

57

Peter Ball 'Demeter'.
mixed media.

"never folksy in the wrong sense", drew on the genius of medieval English stone masonry and ecclesiastical sculpture which first moved him during school trips to great cathedrals. Ball's scouring junk shops for objects with metamorphic potential also recalled Picasso and through him a Spanish genius for metamorphosis. Such qualities flew in the face of Reformation iconoclasm giving Ball's work a richness of symbol and depth of metaphor that chimed well with Banting's eclecticism. This was built on what Blakeston determined was the artist's "sensitivity to respond to ideas in the air".

During June large and small sculpture comprising stone and wood carvings, slate plaques and bronze castings by Oxford-educated and Shropshire-based Anthony Twentyman (b.1906) filled the ground floor in what seemed to reviewer Jenny Stein an "over-cluttered display... practically a retrospective".[37] This was accompanied upstairs by Patricia Allen's 'Persian and Animal Paintings' among which the pictographic 'The Reluctant Bridegroom' and 'We're Just Good Friends' (featuring monkeys on trees) were described by Stein as 'witty paintings on patterned silk". But Stein's estimation of streamlined, elegant abstract sculpture that was "modest, unassuming and made with loving care" set the tone that month. Stein also encapsualated Parr's essential virtue as gallerist in terms of an ongoing story of support, loyalty and commitment to her artists whose work she marketed for intrinsic aesthetic, rather than purely investment, reasons. "Bond Street Galleries", Stein wrote "could take note of her enthusiastic attitude towards her artists and their work".

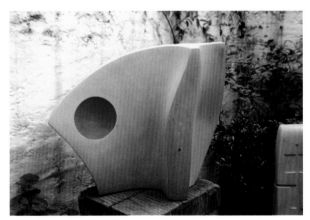

Anthony Twentyman Stone Sculpture in courtyard, June 1974.
Photo: Mary Lambert.

During the high summer season Parr hung works on paper in diverse media by a dozen artists to create a display that Wykes-Joyce described as "one of the best current shows in London".[38] Some big names featured; drawings by Ivon Hitchens, Sutherland,

David Evans 'The Guest'.
oil.

Léger, Moore, Hayden, Nicholson, Pasmore and Nolan were accompanied by two Frink bronzes, John Piper's 'Cartoon for the Baptistry Window, Coventry' and a diverse mix of contemporary sculptors including regulars like Mitchell, Lovell, Adams and Twentyman from the abstract and Ball and Plazzotta from the figurative side. Parr's penchant for sculpture saw a September exhibition of these artists put on in conjunction with the gallery at Buxton Mill, Norwich.

The David Evans exhibition in September featured over 30 medium-sized, flatly painted landscapes depicting empty roads and solitary figures. Parr returned from the big name extravaganza of summer to focus on a contemporary. The Magrittean 'The Visitor' and 'The Guest', featuring interiors with enigmatic figures and empty tables, contained the frozen narrative and Hitchcockian suspense of not only Magritte but Caulfield, Hopper, 1960s Hockney and Jeffrey Edwards. The metaphysical stillness and inscrutability of both interiors and open landscapes was a function of immaculate design, razor-sharp delineation and photo-like accuracy of image formation for which Evans did, however, use his imagination rather than the episcope of photo realist art. These memorable paintings were accompanied by Goldsmith-trained Geoffrey Eastop's ceramic wall hangings and dishes. Eastop's collaboration with John Piper in Henley and exterior ceramic mural for Maudsley Hospital, London provided the credentials for *the* artist potter par excellence. The gallery's undoubted flair for showing diverse ceramicists on an equal and compatible footing with fine artists was evident once again.

Geoffrey Eastop 'Large Orange Dish'.
ceramic.

The October John Milne exhibition comprising 30 sculptures, mainly recent bronzes, and 7 reliefs was highly successful, vindicating 1974 as one of the most productive years of the sculptor's output. Allusion to landscape or maritime themes dominated this output; a return to figurative subjects, which would characterise the final three year's work, was only apparent in 'Athena' and 'Oneiros' both of which the artist wrote in private notes in early 1978 "appear to be watching or surveying". The expansive landscape conception of 'Todra', 'Landscape (Isfahan)' and 'Atlas 11' (1974) reflected the artist's extensive north African and middle eastern travels (in 1973, an unproductive year Milne made two visits to Morocco). The sliced channels of 'Atlas', 'Lemenja', 'Corinthos' and 'Chrysalis' (1974) became a stylistic signature tune, a direct outcome of Milne's topographical experiences in Greek or Moroccan or Persian gorges and narrow vallies.

Both J.P. Hodin's exhibition catalogue essay and Michael Goedhuis' sympathetic review in 'Studio International' indicated Milne's success in laying aside the ghost of Hepworth and establishing an independent voice. The 'Herald Tribune' noted that "his voice is uniquely his own".*39 Hodin saw the influence of Hepworth as positive, a salutary factor allowing one receptive artist to develop from, and build on, the achievements of another. Goedhuis' preference for the centrepiece sculpture 'Credo' (1974), illustrated on the catalogue cover, seemed to be on account of its greater degree of minimal abstraction. 'Credo' "succeeds better than most", Goedhuis wrote, in its avoidance of "literal allusions to antique subject-matter or location".*40 Its austere, pared down surfaces and slight asymmetric 'lean' exemplified what the painter critic Denis Bowen described as "those principals, so associated with

John Milne exhibition Marjorie Parr Gallery, October 1974.
Photo: Peter Kinnear.

St Ives, where precision of craftsmanship and simplicity of form are structurally compounded".*41 Milne later bore this out by stating in 1978 that 'Credo' and its subsequent kindred pieces like 'Resurgence' (1976) and 'Supplication' (1978) achieved a perfect balance where "nothing more could be added to, or taken away from" the final image.

The success of the Parr exhibition owed much to Allan Dunn who, along with Tommy Rowe, provided much help in preparing the rough bronze casts after their return from either the Art Bronze Foundry in Chelsea or the Morris Singer in Basingstoke, Hampshire. Rowe, as we have seen, also worked for other Marjorie Parr artists Denis Mitchell and Breon O'Casey, and also came to show his own work at Parr's St Ives branch.

What Denis Bowen described as the "modulated monumentality" of Milne's freestanding sculptures gave way, during November, to very different fauve-influenced landscape paintings by Eardley Knollys (b.1902). Knollys' instinct for colour, described by the

Eardley Knollys 'La Gariote'.
oil.

eminent reviewer and later 'Burlington Magazine' editor Richard Shone as "arbitary and high in key",[*42] yielded landscapes like 'La Gariote' and 'French Farmhouse' whose structures were less linear than chromatic. Such landscapes, preferred by Shone to the accompanying still life subjects, were "tautly conceived and full of atmosphere" possessing "a potent quality of revelation". The one-time art dealer Knollys' links to the art establishment - during the 1950s and early 1960s he was a member of the Executive Committee of the Contemporary Art Society - stood him in good stead, a late start applauded both by Shone and by Duncan Grant, no less, the Bloomsburyite giving Knollys a gilt-edged accolade when describing him as "one of the purest painters I know".[*43]

The quirky ideographic paintings of Andrew Lanyon followed in December. The eldest son of the revered late Cornish painter Peter (1918-64), Andrew was a recent convert to painting having studied at the London School of Film Technique and experimented with photography and photomontage during the 1960s. Not altogether unlike that of his late father, however, Andrew's work contained what Barbara Wright described as "a complicated mixture of geometric and primitive styles, plus a pinch of underivative surrealism".[*44] The inherently graphic quality of Andrew Lanyon's paintings like 'Tea Break' departed though from Peter's full-bodied expressionism. Following a maiden London solo at the Archer Gallery the previous year the Andrew Lanyon display in the Lower Gallery was accompanied by another Patrick Hall exhibition in which the artist's "special gift for atmospheric watery reflections" did not preclude a number of architectural subjects including depictions of San Marco, Venice, Sicilian villages and the cathedrals at Rheims and Chartres.

Andrew Lanyon 'Tea Break'.
mixed media.

Autumn 1974 was therefore one of the most commercially successful periods for the gallery, Mary Lambert writing during spring 1975 to Alan and Mo

Patrick Hall 'Sicilian Village'.
watercolour.

David and Inga Gilbert with Marjorie Parr.

Frank Doubleday with Barbara Hepworth.
Photo: Marjorie Parr.

Gise, prominent American clients and regular patrons (Gise had been a senior diplomat at the United States Embassy), about the previous year's successes. Lambert recalled the David Evans "a tremendous success",*45 the John Milne show "far better than any of his others" while the Hall exhibition "was no exception" to his usual sell-out. The early part of 1975 was quiet, however, Marjorie and her staff going down with flu. Furthermore Marjorie was involved in a car accident at Hyde Park Corner which Lambert told Gise left her "very shocked and bruised for a week or so".*46

By March business had picked up again and the recent appointment of David Gilbert to run the gallery proved, initially at least, successful, Lambert again telling the Gises that "David Gilbert is fitting into the gallery terribly well and we cannot now imagine what life was like without him... it does mean that Marjorie is a little more free and does not have so many pressures to worry about". Gilbert's seamless transformation from gallery client to director was a reminder of the old adage that an art dealer is only as good as his or her clients. Marjorie had plenty of those, among the more significant of whom were Frank Doubleday of John Players Nottingham, Stanley Picker, the founder of Gala of London, Sheridan Russell who started the organisation Paintings in Hospitals, Leicestershire Education Committee, the Oxford-educated stockbroker Dick Allen, Alan and Mo Gise from the United States Embassy, an interior designer Sheila Sorley, Maurice Lambert and his wife the art historian Rosemary, Rodney and Pam Giesler - keen buyers of John Hitchens, John Christopherson, Douglas Portway and Denis Mitchell - and A.F.C. 'Derek' Turner.

'Selena' and related painting.
Photo: Rodney Giesler.

In common with so many Marjorie Parr Gallery buyers Derek Turner was a friend as well as regular client. Shortly after Turner's death in October 1969 the 'Art and Antiques Weekly' reported that this

John Christopherson 'Buildings near Cape Cornwall'.
oil.
Photo: Charles Allen.

distinguished collector "never liked being referred to as a patron" and "believed in buying from living artists".*47 True to this philanthropic outlook Turner invited artists to his Paddington mews house to see treasures accumulated, the journal added, by a free spirit "totally unaffected by art fashion and the investment side of art buying." Stanley Picker, too, bought to keep, his massive collection of sculpture preserved in perpetuity through the Stanley Picker Trust and housed in a purpose-built gallery at Kingston Hill, Surrey. Marjorie Parr's main sculptors - Lovell, Mitchell, Milne and Plazzotta - accordingly entered the Picker collection. Harley Carpenter and Geoffrey Walker added to their large pot collection. And Dick Allen, who only started collecting in 1969, aged 43, went on to follow up the initial acquistion of John Christopherson's 'Buildings near Cape Cornwall' with purchases of sculpture by Plazzotta, Lovell, Twentyman, Mitchell and Milne. Allen owed his collection to Marjorie's guidance, recalling how "she literally taught me how to look at pictures and sculpture".*48 Indeed after leaving the gallery Marjorie continued to do business with Allen, selling him an Ivon Hitchens. Allen subsequently acquired sculpture by Frink and Hepworth through the Alwin Gallery, where Marjorie had become a consultant.

Aart van Kruiselbergen's exhibition of recent paintings in March 1975 galvanised Gilbert's new directorship of the gallery. The flat, hard edge colour of 'Gone to Lunch', reproduced on the card, relayed a simplified, symmetrical beach composition centred on the incidentals of sun umbrella, deckchairs, beachball, spade and towels. Ivor Francis described the Dutchman's work as "effective and decorative" in the 'Advertiser'*49 for which graphic directness and caricatural wit was responsible. The focus on one of Marjorie's stable of contemporaries was complemented by a group display 'Sculpture and Drawings' on the first and second floors and among many interesting and distinguished sculptors were Adams, Eisenmeyer, Chadwick, McWilliam as well as Jesse Watkins, Margaret Lovell and Ann Christopher.

Recent paintings forming a first solo exhibition for Ewen Henderson followed in April. The Staffordshire-born potter, who worked for a timber firm in Cardiff before studying at Goldsmiths and then, crucially, under Coper and Rie at Camberwell, returned from ceramics to painting at this moment. Watercolours of the Dordogne and other rural idylls formed subject-matter of a rustic kind. Shlomo Cassos' exhibition 'Paintings and Tapestries' on another floor exchanged Henderson's pastoralism for an emblematic emptiness, Peter Stone declaring in the 'Jewish Chronicle' that Cassos' work "looks a bit empty at first because it is very economical" but the "sense of pattern is perfect".*50 During May another telling contrast, this

Edward Piper 'Drawing', 1975.
ink.

time between a painter and sculptor - Edward Piper and Denis Mitchell - was on offer. Bath Academy and Slade-trained Piper, a photographer and designer as well as painter, sprung from a distinguished art family and as such once again revealed Marjorie's promotion of the work of the offspring of established artists. The Mitchell sculptures, including the lignum carving 'Argos' and slate 'Skiddaw', presented work in a multiplicity of materials to reveal the Cornish-based artist's craftsmanly versatility.

The Bloomsburyite Angelica Garnett's 'Pastels' exhibition took place during June. Born into the charmed Bloomsbury circle, Garnett (b.1918) again reflected Marjorie's penchant for heritage and social connection. 'Adonis on the Windowsill' cohered with the tranquil domestic vision of Bell and Grant, the Islington-based Garnett's visits to paint in Sussex tempered by a Euston Road rigour. The contre-jour view balanced foreground domestic shadow with the beckoning reflected light of a Charleston pond. Another Sussex artist, James Hussey, created a more contemporary figuration employing visual tricks and graphic devices like trop l'oeil, mirror distortions and diminishing perspectives as in 'Green Memory'.

The high summer blockbuster 'Scottish Paintings and Drawings' '1775-1975' witnessed the apogee of the Marjorie Parr Gallery's involvement with art north of the border. Cameron, Eardley, Gillies, Peploe, Redpath, Ferguson, Philipson and Michie were all there though not in a loud or clannish way, William Packer describing "in general private and modest work rather than declamatory, and the quality is high".*51 Packer's definition of Scottishness rested on an "honest academicism... an admirable curiosity about developments elsewhere... the colour, and its expressive use". Packer continued his thesis of Scottishness as recently as October 2008 in a 'Guardian' obituary for John Houston. Here he described modern Scottish painting as "direct in the statement, rich in colour and the actual stuff of the paint as it rests on the surface".*52 Colour also breathed life into Tom Davison's acrylic pictures like 'Corfu Landscape', 'Boats at St Ives' and 'St Michael's Mount' to such an extent that the 'Chelsea Post' spoke of "one of the brightest exhibitions held for some time".*53 Enamel plaques and mixed media paintings by Israeli Ruth Neeman accompanied Davison's work during September.

A routine Plazzotta exhibition, his fifth and final solo with Marjorie Parr, included the recumbent 'Young Dancer' and 'Rearing Stallion'. Landscapes on paper by Eardley Knollys accompanied the sculptures, Knollys' ability to extract abstract pattern, à la Hayden, and colour rhythm from flowing landscape topography providing a lyricism to complement Plazzotta's

Angela Garnett 'Adonis on the Windowsill'.
pastel.

anatomic analysis. A major Douglas Portway solo in November contained abstract imagery of subtlety, the atmospheric mystery of Rothko or late Gottlieb balanced with the systematic linear divisions and geometric symmetry of Newman or early Stella. 'Four White Screens' (1973) acquired from Parr by Dick Allen, posited subtle rectilinear ripples within an expansive 'field' of luminous silver-like light. The catalogue described Portway's work in terms of "a synthesis of the classical and the romantic, the conscious and the unconscious: paintings which are both formal and free". Figurative temperas by Central School-trained Luis Canizares accompanied the Portways. The Ruskin School-trained Christian Brett's landscapes and still lifes formed a December display alongside French watercolours by Patrick Hall and sculpture clocks by Robert Scott Simon.

Ivon Hitchens 'South West Edge', 1970.
oil.
Purchased by Dick Allen from Marjorie Parr.
Photo: Charles Allen.

Chapter Five
Under New Management 1976-1981

January 1976 started with 'Paintings, Sculpture and Drawings '1920-75'. Further evidence of the gallery providing an historically diverse range of modern master, as well as contemporary artists, this exhibition won something-for-everyone plaudits and even a healthy income during a traditionally quiet time of year. Peter Ball's 'Primitive Sculpture' alongside Pier Steensma's 'Sleep' (works on paper based on Indian and French themes) which followed in February, although reverting back to the strictly contemporary exhibition, provided evidence galore of traditional ethnic values converging with up-to-the-minute stylistic imperatives.

For Dutch-born and Rotterdam-trained Steensma (b.1939) this entailed the flat colour, abstracted background and hard-edge foreground figuration of fellow Dutchman van Kruiselbergen and David Evans. For Ball a complex liaison between the craftsmanly idiosyncrasies of medieval stonemasonry and ecclesiastical carving on the one hand and what the artist's exhibition statement called "the innocence and spontaneity" of the moderns Miro and Dubuffet acheived an artistic distinctiveness. Steensma's interest in Indian culture took root during the 1960s when he first taught printmaking at Punjab University and later lived in Nepal. Returning to Europe and living in Paris at the time of the 1970 show, Steensma described his work as "an attempt to express a longing for the realisation of the basic inner tranquility of man, as felt while observing people asleep in south India".

Peter Eugene Ball 'Master Gerhard'.
mixed media.

Ball's 'Master Gerhard', a head and torso carrying a tray bearing a model cathedral, was illustrated on the card for what was his fourth solo Parr show. An irrepressible appetite for metamorphosis saw him scour antique shops, markets and beaches for 'found' objects either used directly or modified within the whimsical neo-primitive figures.

Recent pictures by James Cumming were accompanied during March by his wife Betty's tapestries. Like Ball enjoying a fourth solo, the Royal Scottish Academician once again displayed a post-cubist modernity in the instance of flattened, silhouetted still life compositions like 'Table Assembly with Rusted Tins', illustrated on the catalogue, 'Dutch Still Life' or 'A Shetlander's Possessions'. Another familiar name, that of John Hitchens, followed in April with a characteristic mix of landscape and flower pictures. The landscapes, among them 'Late Summer, Harvest Evening' and 'Early Autumn, Morning Haze', registered time of day or season in palpable terms.

James Cumming 'Table Assembly with Rusted Tins', 1976. oil.

But Hitchens' sweeping topographies transcended atmosphere and naturalism to posit an autonomous abstraction indebted to de Stael, De Kooning, Hoffman or Heron while anticipating younger artists like Alan Gouk and Peter Hoida. Imaginary sea compositions by Boston-born and Rhodes Island-trained Andrew Walsh accompanied the Hitchens, the American's Lincolnshire domicile at the time reflected in the work as much as Sussex inhabited the landscapes of his co-exhibitor.

Animal carvings in the vein of Sven Berlin and Anita Mandl by the Buffalo-born Jane Armstrong continued the gallery's cosmopolitan and eclectic contemporary programme. Trained at the Pratt Institute and the Arts Student League in New York, Armstrong described in the exhibition statement that her "goal is to harmonise subject and stone without losing the special movement or animal essence which first capture attention". Influenced by working marble from the Vermont mountains Armstrong, consciously or not, pursued a rich tradition informed by indiginous Eskimo and early modern sculpture by Epstein and Gaudier. Indeed, Armstrong's even-handed deployment of figurative association (with animals) and abstract significance (of the material) yielded a vital and winning tension between form and content. 'Reef Dweller', a fish in veined Italian marble, utilised the internal textures of the marble to enhance and give weight to the streamlined finish of the piece. Phillipa Denby (b.1938) provided an accompanying display of landscape pictures of the Somerset coast whose renowned 'Levels' "with its open skies and changing moods" emulated the breezy, plein-air topographicalities of Hitchens. 'Trees Sedgemoor' from the card, pitted an iconic foreground tree against a starkly flat landscape.

During June, a John Piper exhibition was put on by arrangement with the Marlborough Gallery. Also that month the gallery had a stand at the International Art Fair, Basel where the work of Douglas Portway and Peter Ball was shown. A large grey-coloured four page A3 document on Ball contained an illustrated essay by Max Wykes-Joyce. This described the essential Englishness of Ball's work as being one based on "honesty, immediacy, whimsical imagination, care for craftsmanship and a passion for the eccentric, the quirkish and the individual". Leading to a high summer display 'European Paintings, Drawings and Graphics' a July exhibition 'Happy Birthdays and Other Paintings' by Dorothy Girouard was shown in the gallery with pots and Greek paintings by Ewen Henderson. Girouard's 'Happy Birthday' on the card bizarrely combined Pop Art super-realism with surreal-like symbolism, the seated semi-nude revealingly exposing through an opened striped robe an egg over the vagina and two dolls against the feet.

Jane B. Armstrong 'Marten IV'. tennessee marble.

Christine Fox 'Gateway'.
mixed media.

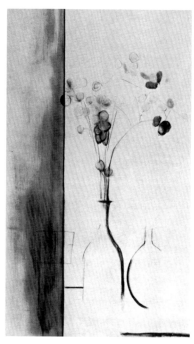

Thelma Hulbert 'Honesty'.
oil.

Experimental modes of contemporary sculpture were exhibited at the gallery at this time, water sculpture by Fleischmann leading in September to 'Christine Fox, Sculpture' (alongside 'Colour Etchings' a display by Madrid-born and Dutch-based Manuel Menan). Bridlington-born and Corsham-trained Fox (b.1922), whose complex bronzes and stone or aluminium assemblages like 'Gateway' and 'Rocking Moon' reflected time spent working in Asia and Africa (she spent 3 months during 1976 apprenticed to an Ashanti gold caster in Ghana) embodied "the relationship between man and his work, the effects shown on man by the tools he uses, the environment with which he works and the influence of the seasons".

Recent paintings by the Bath-born Euston Roader Thelma Hulbert (b.1913) displayed during October were complemented by Michel Kuipers' ceramic sculpture, an interdisciplinary development within the medium of fired clay that was becoming a preferred, even popular, option among contemporary ceramicists influenced by Camberwell, Ewen Henderson and others. Hulbert, who taught throughout the 1960s at the Central School, incorporated measured and disciplined drawing within the ostensibly structured, rigorous compositions. 'Honesty' for example - a large oil on paper reproduced on the card - represented a Coldstreamian delineation of bottle and flowers.

A David Backhouse sculpture display in November, which included a trademark 'Horse and Rider' on the card and a study of tumbling figures 'Free Fall', was placed alongside Jeff Hoare's fourth solo with the gallery. A busy year concluded with 30 Patrick Hall watercolours (1974-76) which provided a spectacle in colour, lyricism and atmospheric subtlety. The Hall exhibition split between architectural 'Façades', among them studies of Chartres, Rheims and San Marco, and 'Landscapes' featuring parallel Norman and Venetian subjects.

A mixed display of gallery artists kickstarted 1977 and led, in February, to a display of Lee Brews paintings and Stage Design drawings by Rhodesia-born Yolanda Sonnabend. South Africa-born Brews, who studied in Johannesburg and Amsterdam before settling in London in 1973, was a compatriot and friend of Douglas Portway and it was no doubt the Portway connection that led to Marjorie's door.

The Brews/Sonnabend exhibition was the last at the old Marjorie Parr Gallery; during March, and much to her chagrin, the gallery's name mutated to Gilbert Parr. While seemingly a compromise the switch left one in no doubt that the new owner, David Gilbert, was now fully in charge, albeit in a way that - in part at least - pursued familiar gallery policies and kept faith

Denis Mitchell 'Sculpture', 1970.
slate.
courtesy Ebe Wharton.

Michael Gillespie '2 up 3 across', 1976.
mixed media.

with established gallery artists. Two such artists, John Hitchens - whose exhibition during March provided evidence of continuity - and Denis Mitchell expressed trepidation at the status quo changes. Mary Lambert, Marjorie's longstanding deputy left at the end of 1976 after a decade, prompting Mitchell to write "I was sad to hear you are leaving, but the wind of change has certainly been blowing down Chelsea way and it is very sad as it will not be the same again". Less than a week later Hitchens, in similar vein, told Lambert that "I just hope it does not flounder without you... Marjorie Parr is the only gallery I know that sends out proper receipts and monthly accounts".[*1] The gallery owed much on that score to the efficient book keeping of Pat Gelley (Sargent), another loyal, committed gallery assistant.

John Hitchens shared the March 1977 slot with Avinash Chandra's recent paintings. Returning to London in the mid 1970s after nearly a decade in New York this cosmopolitan Indian-born artist had formerly enjoyed solos with the Hamilton and South Molton Galleries, London, as well as with Bear Lane, Oxford and Arnolfini, Bristol. Chandra's appearance, together with that of sculptor Michael Gillespie's bronzes and Bernard Stern's ink wash drawings in April, represented new directions, all three artists being the choice of Gilbert rather than Parr. Stern (b.1920), the elder of the two, was a wartime émigré and a founder of the lighting firm 'Rotaflex'. Like Chandra, Stern had enjoyed notable solos - in this case with Drian and John Whibley - before alighting on Gilbert Parr. The distinguished critic J.P. Hodin, who owned several Sterns, described "a semi-abstracted conception between a pure poetic musicality and a mysticism of nature". Hammersmith-trained Gillespie (b. 1929) specialised in bronze casting, a technique he mastered through working for (among others) Jacob Epstein. In 1969 he co-authored (with John Mills) 'Studio Bronze Casting' and later taught at East Anglian art colleges. 'Dish' and 'Two Up Three Across' (1976) featured residual figure or bird subjects on rough stone bases.

Unlike Gillespie and Stern, Patricia Allen exhibited with Marjorie in 1974 before the hand-over to Gilbert. This earlier exhibition 'Persian Paintings and Animals' contained an eye-catching exoticism continued in her May 1977 show 'Paintings 1976-7', which included the Rousseauesque 'Forest Primeval Series' featuring a tiger in large dense foliage. Such subjects reflected not her studies at Birmingham School of Art but her time domiciled thereafter in the Far East. Together with pictures by Hastings-born Paul Fowler and beach-scapes from Norfolk-born and Central School-trained John Bond, the gallery offered much stylistic and thematic variety.

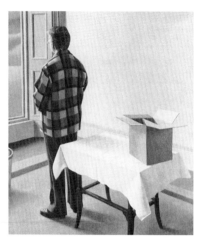

David Evans 'Stormy Weather'.
oil.

In common with Hoare, Ball and Cumming, David Evans also enjoyed a fourth solo with the gallery, an achievement that vindicated both his ongoing commercial appeal and relevance to both Parr and Gilbert. Among the 26 Magritte-influenced pictures the former Granada Arts Fellow offered the enigmatic 'Stormy Weather', 'The Perfect Stranger' and 'The Traveller', pictures with solitary individuals often with their backs turned looking out of a window or into a mirror as if into another world. Evans' flirtations with Americana were also evident in a manner revealing less the influence of Magritte than of Hopper. 'California Gas', 'Orange County Freeway' and 'Flags and Hills, Utah' clearly derived from the artist's travels across the Western States, experiences that perhaps evoked d'Archangelo and Hockney as much as Hopper.

Barbara Rae 'Lilypool'.
oil.

The Edinburgh-trained Scot Barbara Rae (b.1943), who enjoyed a September solo, continued the gallery's association with Scottish art, links that, when one also takes into account the strong presense of a St Ives contingent under Marjorie, amounted to a significant celtic dimension within the gallery's history. Rae's catalogue text indeed referred to "the darkness and romance of the Celt" and described the large rock paintings on display as reflecting "the mysticism and loneliness of standing stones". Rae's later success never obscured the importance of what was her first solo London exhibition. She recalled being aware "that many of my former teachers at Edinburgh College were exhibiting with Marjorie Parr so I reasoned that she might favour an approach from a young Scottish artist. I boldly went to London, and without a prior telephone call or letter, arrived at the gallery. David Gilbert did look a bit bored so I think that he took pity on the naive out-of-towner... looking through my very dark slides he said "I will give you a show". I was

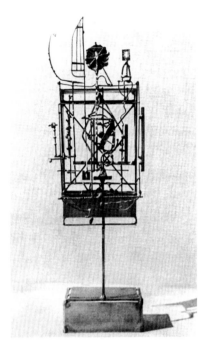

Richard Blomfield 'Defined Space'.
steel.

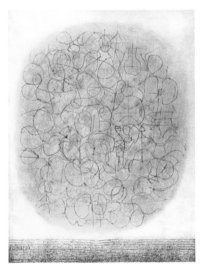

Douglas Portway 'Untitled', 1977.
oil on paper.

overjoyed and a bit surprised. I will always be thankful for the opportunity to show at the Gilbert/Parr Gallery. It was a pity that I was never able to meet Marjorie".*2

Rae's exact contemporary, the Swiss-born Barcelo, exhibited gouache and ink paintings in an adjacent gallery space, 'Blue Moonlight' offering, within differing stylistic terms, a similar feeling of mystery and romance. Shlomo Cassos' 1975 maiden Marjorie Parr exhibition 'Paintings and Tapestries' was now followed by a small display of oil pastels and etchings that accompanied a fifth solo Peter Ball sculpture exhibition. Like 'Cut-Away Horizon' in the 1975 show Cassos' 'Gestation', featured on the card, simplified a natural motif to near minimal abstraction, deploying a reduced table-like foreground structure against a flat, uniformly-coloured background suggestive of a landscape horizon with hazy, indistinct sun.

The sculptor Richard Blomfield's exhibition 'Structures and Situations' accompanying Douglas Portway paintings (on canvas and paper) followed in November; both shared an allusive form of abstraction relaying figurative source material in the sculptor's case and landscape in the painter's. Guildford and Slade-trained Blomfield (1930-2007) taught during the early 1960s at Bath Academy of Art, Corsham Court before becoming Director of Art at Cheltenham Boys College. Mechanical totem-like welded metal pieces like the Miroesque 'Family Group', 'Defined Space' and 'Waiting Group' also recalled the small, thin, upright figurines of Giacometti. The whimsicality of these figures situated within scaffolding had a graphic basis originating from drawings and paintings. While inviting subjective responses and a diversity of interpretations Blomfield also insisted on urban influences gleaned from London and Cheltenham. On the card he talked about the "formality and informality of townscape with landscape, spaces organised and confirmed by landmarks and planned continuities, the movement of people, the flight of birds" as inspiring and influencing the sculpture. Portway's 'Untitled' on the card remained a more cryptic image though the large yellow oval bearing writhing biomorphic lines and striations on a cream background suggested a primitivist vision of the sun as a primordial source of energy and giver of life.

The year ended with a significant Margaret Neve exhibition comprising over three dozen pictures among which was 'Sheep in the Rocks' illustrated on the card. These were complemented by Ivo Mosley pots. Wolverhampton-born Neve (b.1929) belonged to an established, cultured Black Country family in which art was encouraged. Studies at first Birmingham and later the Royal Academy Schools, London under Bernard Fleetwood Walker instilled an early technical facility. What the critic Sister Wendy Beckett later

71

*Margaret Neve 'Sheep in the Rocks'.
oil.*

termed the "ruthless control" of a "dauntingly tight" style applied to the later imaginative work; the early student work focused instead on the 'workshop of the world' - that compelling, early industrial landscape between Wolverhampton and Birmingham which she encountered every day. Neve drew the towpaths and canals for worked-up studio pictures that retained an element of industrial realism throughout the student period. After leaving the R.A. in 1951 she participated in group shows with Roland, Browse and Delbanco and taught at L.C.C. evening classes, auspicious developments that were, however, to be put on hold by what she described as the "crucial turning point" of her marriage to the engraver James Sutton in 1955.

An interlude raising a family led, during the mid 1970s, to a new and very different religious and visionary style employing a kind of 'spiritual' pointillism or mosaic-like painted patterns to achieve a sublime, arcadian and symbolic vision. This change had perhaps been informed by early experiences of local museums, notably the Barber Institute and Birmingham City Museum and Art Gallery where Pre-Raphaelitism was prominent and whose inimitable mid-Victorian style rubbed off. A scholarship to Italy introduced her to early Florentine and Siennese paintings. Neve's mature idiosyncratic style also drew on the job illustrating children's books for Macmillans. The acquisition of a holiday home in north-west Wales where, as she put it, "the spiritual and the visual started to come together"*3 had a further impact, Neve becoming a latter-day non-Welsh artist - in the footsteps of Wilson, Turner, Herman and Sutherland - enraptured by the Principality's romantic landscape. Neve's almost human characterisation of sheep owed much to close encounters through her exposed cottage window.

Byron Temple 'pot with handle'.

72

John Milne 'Birdsong', 1975. bronze.

The approach to Marjorie was made on Neve's behalf by Sutton. She liked a composition of a hare at night and showed some small works in the basement in 1976. This led to two major exhibitions under David Gilbert both of which were successful and launched her late exhibition career. Another artist who straddled the Parr/Gilbert divide was Pier Steensma whose exhibition 'Watercolours from India and Tunisia' continued the transcendental preoccupations of the previous exhibitions with Marjorie on buddhist or sleep themes. Vivien Lowenstein found the display "preoccupied with the 'beyond' - the happening on the other side", and, more specifically, she described how the dominant tent or screen motif "is used to define and carry us over the brink between the conscious and subconscious".[4] Such interests were timely and in sync with the generational zeitgeist, the precise vedic science of consciousness (along with its coronary yogic practise) being promulgated and extended at that time beyond the 1960s counter-culture to reach middle-class and middle-age suburbia.

Glyn Morgan's spring exhibition of paintings, collages and drawings drew less on the orient than on classical myth, specifically the Orpheus theme, which Michael Ford found "gentle, enticingly involving".[5] Previous solo exhibitions at the Drian (1969) and Richard Demarco Galleries (1973) and at the Gardner, Sussex University (1974) culminated in the Gilbert Parr exhibition which proved successful enough to warrant a second one during spring 1980.

The John Milne exhibition during late April and early May was supported by a display of pots by Byron Temple, a one-time Leach Pottery employee in

John Milne working at Meridian Bronze Foundry, January 1977.
Photo: Ian Erskine.

St Ives, and Goldsmiths and Slade-trained Geoffrey MacEwan's watercolours. The Milne catalogue, unusually lavish for the period, contained a cover illustration of the Brancusian 'Birdsong'. Coming barely 6 weeks before the sculptor's unexpected death the exhibition contained signs not of an endgame but rather of a new departure into minimal, architecturally-inspired forms summarised in Guy Burn's review as "clear and concise distillations in the abstract idiom".[6] 'Brooklyn (or Surf Forms)', 'Cheops' (1977), 'Sakkara (Egyptian City)', 'Pyramids' and 'Dhows' (1978) - the latter pair probably never cast from the plaster prototypes - epitomised these new and sadly unresolved developments. The artist's catalogue statement about attempting to achieve "light, simplicity above all space and freedom and love" was reflected in the spare polished geometric forms that partly made up the exhibition. The inspiration of ancient Islamic or pre-classical architecture also for once gave way to the modern in 'Brooklyn', whose simple thrusting spans related to recent American travels (he had exhibitions in Philadelphia and Kentucky during the previous autumn) and the experience of the Brooklyn, Williamsburg or Golden Gate bridges.

Burn also referred to the importance of Milne's drawings, describing "vortexes and corridors slashed out of the picture plane with bold finality". Such observations chimed with Barbara Hepworth's early admonition to Milne that "when your sculpture is as good as your drawing you will have arrived". The large, sweeping charcoal drawings, while echoing both reliefs and forms in the round, were not - in distinction to small, unexhibited pen diagrams - studies for them.

Throughout June recent paintings (acrylics and watercolours) of Salisbury Cathedral, Greenwich, Venice and Regents Park, London - all reflecting a penchant for timeless, clichéd or art historically-loaded subjects and for what the reviewer Beatrice Phillpots described as a Monetesque "concern with the changing qualities of the light"[7] - by the architect-trained painter Norah Glover held their own for a month in the gallery. A John Whibley Gallery stalwart

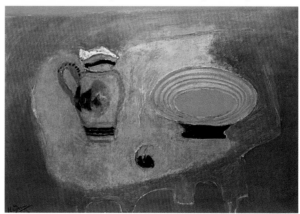

Henri Hayden 'Pot et Plat Rond', 1966.
oil.

74

- she enjoyed no fewer than 8 solos in the Cork Street Gallery between 1962 and 75 - Glover offered both relevant architectural expertise and seasoned experience as a much exhibited painter. The 'Financial Times' critic H. Brockman spoke of how her "professional qualifications as an architect have enabled her to give complete authenticity to her subjects but at the same time a deep sensitivity is infused into the chosen technique of acrylic painting where light and depth are conveyed through an overall atmosphere of great delicacy". A pastoral scene, (rather than concrete architectural subject) 'Thames Poplars', reproduced on the card, revealed what Phillpots observed was Glover's ability "to create a dreamlike impression".

The Slade-trained art school teacher Michael Wharton's (b.1933) exhibition during July also characterised the behaviour of light to "erode, modify or mollify concrete form", reviewer Richard Walker explaining how, even in close-up focus still life, Wharton's objects were realised "as areas of thickened light, matrices of light mysterious and elusive, not as areas of unyielding matter".*8 This was reflected in Jack Lindsay's catalogue note; "colour and form are realised in terms of movement... reveals a sense of wholeness, of the vital integration of object, light, colour, space". The catalogue cover, containing an image of 'Wave Breaking with Spray', certainly relayed qualities of movement and "the vital integration" of descriptive and abstract, naturalistic and plastic use of paint.

David Gilbert continued Marjorie's policy of airing major modern masters, invariably represented by more accessibly priced prints, drawings or small works, during the high summer season. 'Paintings and Drawings of Distinction 1951-78' was no exception by including old favourite Henri Hayden, whose orange and green 'Pot et Plat Rond' (1966) illustrated the card, Pasmore, Piper, Scott, Wells as well as more recent artists like Portway, Kate Nicholson and Donald Hamilton Fraser. A feeling of *déja vu* did not detract from a group of collectable delights which led, during October, back to the routine contemporary exhibition, now featuring a sculptor Christine Fox and a painter Andrew Lanyon.

Between them, contrasting architectonic and dreamscape imagery were on offer. Max Wykes-Joyce's view that "reality, fantasy and dreams are inextricably mingled"*9 in Lanyon's surreal-inspired work put Fox's indoor and outdoor metal sculptures on the spot. These functioned as a site specific object as in the case of a fountain piece, or as intricate structures, embodying both formalist and metaphorical significance. Lanyon's second exhibition at the gallery was firmly within the David Gilbert era though his association with Marjorie stemmed from her St Ives

James Campbell 'Ball'.
ceramic.

Andrew Lanyon 'The Thriller'.
oil.

gallery, from her personal charm and from her penchant for dealing in the work of the offspring of famous or established artists. Lanyon remembered an easy working relationship where there were as he put it "no problems"*10 and this extended to the less charismatic Gilbert's tenure as director.

The acute, even photo real verisilimitude of Neil Dallas Brown's erotic nudes took the metaphysical mystery of Evans and van Kruiselbergen towards what Guy Burn described as a "chillingly dead-pan realism".*11 The lurid sexual atmosphere of brothels was evoked by recumbent, anonymous females guarded by a dog or parrot. Burn's estimation that these "symbols with their overtones of bestiality give a stifling sense of imprisonment in a sour-sweet sexual obsession" would surely not have gelled with Marjorie. Ceramics by Eton-trained James Campbell accompanied Brown's paintings. Patrick Hall followed like a breath of fresh air immediately afterwards. Guy Burn also reviewed Hall's more salubrious watercolour exhibition describing "those conventional

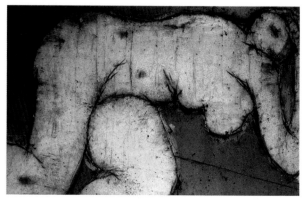

John Emanuel 'The Nude', 1978.
oil.

subjects which are well suited to the medium at its wettest; estuaries at low tide and river scenes".*12 The occurance of continental, as well as British, subject-matter did not confuse the perceptive and well-informed Burn who, while finding "gay and gallic" Seine views indebted to Marquet and Sisley, reverted to type by concluding that Hall's were "nevertheless firmly rooted in the British watercolour tradition".

During the early weeks of 1979 Gilbert exhibited first India ink drawings by Ibiza-born Antonio Mari Ribas (1906-74) then Lee Brews paintings and Michael Gillespie bronzes during February. Ribas' ink drawings, produced with a broad bamboo pen, contained "an immediacy reminiscent of Goya and Rembrandt" according to the exhibition card. Gillespie's bronzes also combined craftsmanly skill with confident, even virtuoso, gesture, the Hammersmith-trained sculptor having cast for Epstein and Frink. A similar confident robustness characterised

John Hitchens 'Flowers Before Summer'.
oil.

powerful and sculptural mixed media drawings of crouched, reclining or standing nudes by Cumbria-born, St Ives-based John Emanuel. The former sign-writer enjoyed on this occasion his first London solo. Julie Lacey discovered densely-worked figures that "convey the idea of mass and a strong sense of design".*13 Emanuel's show was a staging post for further solos at Montpelier Studio, Knightsbridge during the next 15 years, Marjorie's friend Bernice Sandelson taking cue from her mentor and importing several St Ives artists, among them Emanuel and Milne, to Montpelier.

Jack B. Yeats 'Safe Harbour', 1946.
oil.

During May what Richard Walker termed John Bond's "calmly enjoyable"*14 figure and beach compositions in the mould of Evans and van Kruiselbergen were exhibited alongside enigmatic structures and box constructions by Inverness-born and

77

Aberdeen-trained Will MacLean. The tradition of vital, instructive contrast between artists was therby perpetuated at the gallery. 'Recent Flower Paintings' in June revealed John Hitchens as a lyric colourist, Vivien Lowenstein describing the artist's intense floral hues in terms of "an intoxicating and ecstatic resonance" within "bold and methodical"*15 compositions. Hitchens told Mary Lambert how this themed exhibition, together with a large mural near Horsham in Sussex, had soaked up his energies during much of the previous year.

A summer season mixed modern master display 'Figurative Paintings, Drawings and Sculpture of Distinction' included Jack Yates' 'Safe Harbour' (1946) as well as Hayden and many others featured in the similarly titled show at the gallery the previous year. Not until after mid September did the gallery present another contemporary solo show, sculpture by Peter Ball accompanied by 'Meditations' comprising Jan Hubertus' tempera and watercolour paintings. Recent works by Douglas Portway followed in November, prompting reviewer Richard Walker to dismiss the idea of Portway being either a bona fide abstract or expressionist painter. Instead Walker found that Portway's oils on paper contained "quite evident symbolic forms analogous to Miro".*16 Notwithstanding the fact that Miro and other European surrealists had inspired American abstract expressionism, Portway's semi-legible symbols composed from nervous ambulent lines and soft discs of colour were more restrained and contemplative than the riotous colour clashes and overt gesturalism of expressionism. Portway was, all the same, one of the earliest painters of his generation to sample the work of Rothko, Kline and Gottlieb in New York during the mid 1950s, the young South African visiting New York on a scholarship and exhibiting his work at the Venice Bienale in 1956.

Among Marjorie's stable Portway was probably best able to conduct a similarly warm working relationship with Gilbert. The artist did, however, struggle through a lean period in early 1979 when Caroline, the artist's wife, confided to Mary Lambert that "Douglas is having great troubles work-wise - one of those 'fallow' times when nothing seems to be emerging - its making him very morose",*17 The works produced for November acquitted themselves well, however, and encouraged Gilbert to continue showing this good painter not only during the gallery's twilight years of 1981 and 1982 but also throughout the later 1980s in the Black Forest, Germany and then during the late 1990s at Gallery Gilbert, Dorchester. Three Portway retrospectives 'Portway in Bristol 1984-93' (April 1997), 'Portway in St Ives 1967-83' (June 1997) and 'Portway: the Years in Spain 1957-66' (planned for spring 1998) in Dorchester proved Gilbert a devoted and effective Portway supporter.

Margaret Neve paintings on wood, together with Ivo Mosley pots completed the 1979 schedule. Vivien Lowenstein saw Neve's sheep compositions as offering continuity of subject writing that "Welsh landscape billows forth in a flood of rich and happy hues". The exaggeration of almost supernatural and Pre-Raphaelitic colour was matched thematically, the personified sheep appearing to Lowenstein to have "human expression and understanding... with a mature and timeless gaze".

Mixed exhibitions by gallery artists filled the walls during the early weeks of 1980. A solo Glyn Morgan exhibition 'Paintings and Collages' during April was inspired by music and divided into 'Fantasies after Mahler' using recurring bird imagery and what Julie Lacey called "romantic fantasies"[*18] based on myth. Richard Blomfield's 'Drawings, Paintings and Sculptures 1977-80' followed in May. This display contained Miroesque whimsy. The totemic 'Hieroglyphic Group' (1978), a welded assemblage of

Patrick Hall 'Auxerre'.
watercolour.

everyday fragments, was deemed to have "developed from a vocabulary of signs and forms evolved from Egyptian as well as more modern sources."

Eighteen new works by David Evans during July revealed the critical relationship between drawing and painting in this meticulous artist's work, Julie Lacey correctly speaking of "a very gifted realist painter".[*19] The closely-toned 'grisaille' of the 1977 exhibition was replaced here, Lacey reported, with "warmer tones in keeping with his current theme, illumination." 'Slow Passage', illustrated in 'Arts Review', characterised the new palette informed by the "deadening light of the flourescent tube, and the warm mellowing glow of tungsten light". An enigmatic interior theme contained a uniformed man - a janitor or security guard perhaps

- pacing down an impersonal, institutional corridor. The strip light bathed the scene in artificial light and the wall clock, at 2.30, remained ambiguously poised between afternoon or early morning. Together with 'North Corridor' and 'Supreme' this work contained mystery, suspense and metaphysical calm.

The high summer slot was again a large mixed display of old and new favourites. During October 1980 the husband and wife pairing of Valerie Thornton and Michael Chase introduced an entirely new note. Thornton's flair for architectural structure evident in the drawings and etchings of the 'Columns and Windows' series and the "exuberant watercolours" of Chase's 'Forest Interiors' theme both amounted to a "distinct personal style"[*20] according to Frances Spalding. Although better known as an influential art administrator Chase had an established record as painter, showing with Zwemmer between 1953 and 1965 and Minories, Colchester between 1966 and 1974. Other notable exhibitions during the gallery's final 18 months included those by Pier Steensma in December 1980, a 36-work Patrick Hall watercolour exhibition using customary French and Venetian subjects in October 1981, followed by a Douglas Portway solo in November. A Clive Soord show in April 1982 anticipated the gallery's closure a few months later, Gilbert and his wife Inga continuing to trade from their German base and exhibiting work, particularly by Peter Ball, Paul Fowler, Will MacLean and Douglas Portway, at Art Fairs.

Chapter Six

The Final Years 1981-2007

During autumn 1974, the transitional period between the Parr and Gilbert régimes at the gallery, Marjorie wrote to Peter Thursby that "David is getting on very well and everybody likes him very much, but having been a solicitor all his life, he finds a Gallery rather bewildering".*¹ As well as undoubtedly smoothing his passage Marjorie also provided invaluable advice and support to Denys Alwin Davis - becoming an official advisory consultant to the Alwin Gallery - and to Bernice Sandelson who opened the Montpelier Studio, Knightsbridge during the late 1970s. Sandelson recalled Marjorie being "wonderfully helpful to me"*² particularly in the instance of being introduced to Margaret Neve, Patrick Hall and John Hitchens. Sandelson also continued Marjorie's St Ives connections, exhibiting Milne and Mitchell as well as launching Rachel Nicholson's exhibition career in London much to her father Ben's delight who saw Rachel's work exhibited there. Through the popular painter and printmaker Patrick 'Rainbow' Hughes the Montpelier also exhibited John Emanuel. Bernice, who came to art dealing not through glass but through running a shortlived cartoon gallery in Kensington (her husband Victor had been a political journalist with the 'Financial Times'), later handed Montpelier to her son Robert who eventually leased it to James Colman and moved into a contemporary, international art market with a relocation to Cork Street. Margaret Neve, from the original Marjorie Parr stable, remained the token survivor at Sandelson's Cork Street gallery.

Marjorie Parr with Aart van Kruiselbergen at the Alwin Gallery.

Robert Sandelson's 1992 obituary on Patrick Hall further underlined his links to Marjorie's artistic stable. Sandelson lamented the disappearance of artists of Hall's ilk but celebrated the York-born painter's "very English compromise between plein air and studio work".*³

It was not only in terms of her experience and expertise but also for her social vivacity and enthusiasm that Marjorie continued, well into old age, to be a welcome presence on the gallery scene. Jilly Knight remembered that from an early stage Marjorie was "always very interested in clothes and loved colour".*⁴ Peter Thursby, whose silver pendant (silversmith Frank Johnson) based on Parr's equestrian logo was made for Marjorie's 80th birthday late in 1986, received a letter from Marjorie telling him that "when I wear it at Patrick Hall's Private View at the Montpelier in October there will be many of my clients there and I am sure they will all notice it and love the idea."

Peter Thursby silver pendant made for Marjorie Parr's 80th birthday.

Another successful gallery enterprise owing a debt to Marjorie was that of the Australian Tim Boon who, after a couple of spells helping hang exhibitions and doing heavy lifting work at the gallery (1968-69) and again during the spring of 1970, went on to open Amalgam, a gallery in Barnes, south-west London specialising in ceramics and original prints during the later 1970s and 1980s. Boon too, remembered Marjorie being "very supportive and encouraging" and "a big personality".[*5] After Amalgam Boon took on ceramicist Tony Birk's Alpha House Gallery, Sherborne in Dorset.

During the long retirement years Marjorie also occupied herself with the Arthritis Research Council and told Peter Thursby late in 1987 that "I am up to my eyes in desk work as I organised a big raffle in aid of Arthritis Research".[*6] In this she was helped by Diane Millin. But her manifold art world friends also kept in touch and among her assistants Mary Lambert and Ebe Wharton remained helpful. After two years at the gallery in the late 1960s Wharton returned to later help at private views and, during the 1970s, stayed a fortnight at Marjorie's Elm Park Gardens flat after Marjorie's hip operation. She also indulged her early interest in music and was a regular concert-goer. A friendship with Cheyne Walk-based Sheridan Russell led to her often more than informal advice on the development of Russell's new project now called 'Paintings in Hospitals'. Not long after her 90th birthday Marjorie elected to go to Meadbank Nursing Centre, Battersea, where she remained for the next 10 years until her death there in May 2007. A 100th birthday party at the Home organised by her nephew Leslie Pollard and his wife, attracted a large number of her family, friends and professional contacts, a testimony to the esteem and respect she earned from a wide variety of people.

The esteem and respect she gained across the entire board - the gallery staff, clients, art dealers, artists and casual acquaintances she came into contact with all loved and trusted her - confirmed a widespread popularity. Perhaps those closest to her - the artists - later spoke in glowing terms about how important a catalyst she had been in their early careers. Some artists like Vivien ap Rhys Pryce and Jeff Hoare had made impromptu approaches straight in off the street and touting their wares. As well as contributing unobtrusively to many group shows under both Parr and Gilbert, ap Rhys Pryce enjoyed the one solo in 1969. She always sold well and the sculptor later recalled that Marjorie "made you feel it was worthwhile to continue"[*7] and that "a good feeling" always pervaded the atmosphere of the gallery. For Aart van Kruiselbergen the approach was less direct, the Dutch painter having first worked for a year at Anthony d'Offay's gallery before helping out at

Marjorie with Geoffrey Walker, 1988.
Photo: Harley Carpenter.

the Marjorie Parr Gallery where he also became a successfull exhibitor. But van Kruiselbergen's verdict on Marjorie was equally decisive referring to how "she changed my life".*8

In similar vein the sculptor Evelyn Williams remembered how Marjorie "was greatly supportive at the beginning of my career and gave me an excellent show."*9 For John Milne and Denis Mitchell this uniquely loyal and supportive dealer remained so until the end of their respective careers, Milne inscribing thanks to Marjorie in his 1977 Hodin monograph for "friendship and years of encouragement", Mitchell

Denis Mitchell in his Newlyn studio, 1974.
Photo: Peter Kinnear.

referring to Marjorie in his 1992 Penwith Society 80th birthday exhibition catalogue as "my Guardian Angel who made it possible for me to produce the work". Artists from further afield with more fleeting or sporadic involvements with the gallery, such as the Edinburgh painter David Michie, were no less impressed, Michie recounting "I liked her and she kindly invited me to exhibit in her gallery from time to time. She was rather an enthusiast and engaging and I was pleased to be part of the exhibitions she presented." And echoing the leading London gallerist Leslie Waddington's estimation that she was "completely correct in business matters".*10 Michie remembered that Marjorie was "very honest in her dealings with me and not at all intimidating".*11

Another Edinburgh-based painter, David Evans, had a similar story to tell, recalling that Marjorie "was so kind and welcoming to me; so easy to work with and letting me arrange pictures as I wanted them. I became very fond of Marjorie too; she even arranged a dinner for me at her flat in Elm Park Gardens with Carel Weight, my old professor at the RCA. Marjorie sold some of my pictures to some well known

Margaret Lovell 'Sorbus Head'.
bronze.
courtesy Porthminster Gallery, St Ives.

people. She had some 'famous' customers. One day during my exhibition there in 1974 I called into the gallery to see Marjorie. She told me she'd had some 'very scruffy' people in the gallery and was going to ask them to leave. They introduced themselves as 'Crosby, Stills, Nash and Young', the pop group, and promptly bought several pictures".*12

Roger Leigh's son Nick, a picture framer and construction-maker who knew Marjorie from an early age recalled the "proper" and "conventional" aspect of a woman who was too old to be directly involved with the youth movement of the time*.13 Others remember that, despite her undoubted charms, she would not suffer fools or countenance nonsense. But she was so much more than an efficient gallery owner and businesswoman, instilling a belief and confidence in her artists, whom she loved, and transferring her faith in, and enthusiasm for, their work to her many clients who actually gained satisfaction from acquiring art through her gallery. Many clients became longstanding friends too, as is evident throughout the history of the gallery. It became as much a community and fellowship as a business venue. The Americans Alan and Mo Gise, who went on to buy the work of Hoare, van Kruiselbergen, Evans, Williams, Portway, Ball and many potters, later spoke of "a lovely relationship with Marjorie"*14 and Dick Allen, an equally regular buyer, recalled that "she literally taught me how to look at pictures and sculpture... I have bought well and that I owe to Marjorie, but money is a minor consideration it was her joire de vivre, her instinctive intuition, her amazing friendliness and the quality of her instruction which I shall remember".*15

These attributes were linked to her longevity, the abstract artist Nigel Van Wieck expressing happiness "that she lived to over 100, this does not surprise me because I never met anyone who had as much vitality as her".*16 Marjorie Parr died at Meadbank on 27th May 2007. A well-attended thanksgiving service was held at St Lukes Church, Chelsea on 1st June 2007.

Margaret Lovell, Simon Hitchens, John Hitchens, Dick Allen, Janet Yapp,
Veronica Franklin, Ebe Wharton and Diane Millin after thanksgiving service.
Photo: Harley Carpenter.

Footnotes

Chapter One

1. *Andrew Lanyon in telephone conversation with the author. April 2008.*
2. *John Hitchens in conversation with the author, Greenleaves, Sussex. April 2007.*
3. *Rebecca West to Marjorie Parr. 28/2/1954.*
4. *Jilly Knight in telephone conversation with the author. 1/7/08.*
5. *Susan Groom 'Arts Review'. 22/8/64.*
6. *Oswell Blakeston 'Arts Review', Vol 16. No 17. Sept 64.*
7. *Susan Groom 'Arts Review'. 17/10/64.*
8. *Eric Newton 'The Guardian'. 20/10/64.*
9. *Susan Groom 'Arts Review'. 15/5/65.*
10. *Susan Groom 'Arts Review'. 12/6/65.*
11. *Susan Groom 'Arts Review'. 18/9/65.*
12. *Lawrence Bradshaw 'Arts Review'. 13/11/65.*
13. *T.G. Rosenthal 'The Listener'. 18/11/65.*
14. *Joanna Borchand 'Arts Review'. 11/12/65.*
15. *Lawrence Bradshaw 'Arts Review'. 22/1/66.*
16. *Cottie Burland 'Arts Review'. 19/2/66.*
17. *'The Kensington Post'. 11/2/66.*

Chapter Two

1. *Susan Groom 'Arts Review'. Feb/March 1967.*
2. *'Arts Review'. 2/9/67.*
3. *Philip Hicks in conversation with the author. 3/7/07.*
4. *John Gainsborough 'Arts Review'. Nov/Dec 1967.*
5. *Richard Walker 'Arts Review'. 20/1/68.*
6. *'Scene' by David Clemens 'Daily Mirror'. 12/6/68.*
7. *Max Wykes-Joyce. Introduction to 'Enzo Plazzotta; a catalogue raisonné'. Trefoil, London 1986.*
8. *Oswell Blakeston 'Plazzotta at Marjorie Parr' 'Arts Review'. 28/9/68.*
9. *John Russell 'Sunday Times'. 23/2/69.*
   Edwin Mullins 'Sunday Telegraph'. 23/2/69.

Chapter Three

1. *Barbara Hepworth. Letter to Marjorie Parr. 13/5/68.*
2. *'St Ives Times and Echo'. 16/4/69.*

3. Barbara Wright 'Arts Review'. Feb 69.

4. Michael Nye 'Arts Review'. April 69.

5. Gerald Smith 'Arts Review'. May 69.

6. Barbara Wright 'Arts Review'. June 69.

7. Richard Walker 'Arts Review'. Sept 69.

Chapter Four

1. Max Wykes-Joyce 'Arts Review'. 14/2/70.

2. Richard Walker 'Arts Review'. March 1970.

3. Jeff Hoare in conversation with the author, Strand on the Green, London. 12/4/07.

4. Brian Hornal 'Outdoor Sculpture' 'Arts Review'. 1970.

5. Marina Vaizey 'Arts Review'. 13/3/71.

6. Cottie Burland 'Arts Review'. 10/4/71.

7. Richard Walker 'Arts Review'. 19/6/71.

8. Richard Walker 'Arts Review'. 20/11/71.

9. Gerald Smith review and Denis Bowen interview with Jesse Watkins. 'Arts Review'. 1972.

10. Marina Vaizey 'Arts Review'.

11. Bernard Denvir 'London Letter', 'Art International', Vol 16/5. 20/5/72.

12. Richard Walker 'Arts Review'. Sept 72.

13. Peter Dyke 'Arts Review'. 20/5/72.

14. Richard Walker 'Arts Review'. 15/7/72.

15. Richard Walker 'Mixed Exhibition'. 'Arts Review'. 12/8/72.

16. Richard Smart 'Arts Review'. 12/10/72.

17. Michael Shepherd 'Arts Review'. 16/12/72.

18. Richard Shone 'Arts Review'. 13/1/73.

19. Karen Usborne 'Arts Review'. 10/2/73.

20. Terence Mullaly 'Evocative use of colour by two artists'. 'Daily Telegraph'. 14/3/73.

21. Michael Shepherd 'Arts Review'. 10/3/73.

22. Max Wykes-Joyce 'Arts Review'. 24/4/73.

23. Richard Walker 'Arts Review'. 16/6/73.

24. Duchess of St Albans 'The Times of Chelsea'. p25. June 1973.

25. Elena Gaputyte written note. 25/6/73.

26. Elena Gaputyte. Letter to the author. 1990.

27. Roy Miles 'Arts Review'. 14/7/73.

28. Brian Wallworth 'Arts Review'. 11/8/73.

29. Max Wykes-Joyce 'International Herald Tribune'. 8/9/73.

30. Timothy Mason 'Arts Review'. 22/9/73.

31. Barbara Wright 'Arts Review'. 15/12/73.

32. Richard Smart 'Arts Review'. 8/2/74.

33. Barbara Wright 'Arts Review'. 8/3/74.

34. Jeff Hoare in conversation with the author, Strand on the Green, London. 12/4/07.

35. Peter Pope 'Arts Review'. 19/4/74.

36. Oswell Blakeston 'Arts Review'. 17/5/74.

37. Jenny Stein 'Arts Review'. 28/6/74.

38. Max Wykes-Joyce 'Arts Review' 26/7/74.

39. 'Herald Tribune'. 19/10/74.

40. Michael Goedhuis 'Studio International'. Nov 1974.

41. Denis Bowen 'Arts Review'. Oct 74.

42. Richard Shone 'Arts Review'. 1974.

43. Duncan Grant. Statement in catalogue.

44. Barbara Wright 'Arts Review'. Dec 1974.

45. Mary Lambert. Letter to Alan and Mo Gise. 3/3/75.

46. ibid.

47. 'Art and Antiques Weekly'. Oct 1969.

48. Dick Allen. Letter to the author. 3/6/07.

49. Ivor Francis 'The Advertiser'. 10/1/75.

50. Peter Stone 'Jewish Chronicle'. 11/4/75.

51. William Packer 'Scottish paintings and drawings' 'Financial Times'. 8/8/75.

52. William Packer 'Guardian'. 3/10/08.

53. 'Chelsea Post'. 3/10/75.

Chapter Five

1. John Hitchens. Letter to Mary Lambert.

2. Barbara Rae. e-mail to the author. 22/9/08

3. Margaret Neve in conversation with the author, London. Spring 2007.

4. Vivien Lowenstein 'Arts Review'. 3/3/78.

5. Michael Ford 'Arts Review'. 31/3/78.

6. Guy Burn 'Arts Review'. 12/5/78.

7. Beatrice Phillpots 'Arts Review'. 9/6/78.

8. Richard Walker 'Arts Review'. 7/7/78.

9. Max Wykes-Joyce 'Arts Review'. 13/10/78.

10. Andrew Lanyon in conversation with the author. 12/6/08.

11. Guy Burn 'Arts Review'. 10/11/78.

12. Guy Burn 'Arts Review'. 8/12/78.

13. Julie Lacey 'Arts Review'. 16/3/79.

14. Richard Walker 'Arts Review'. 25/5/79.

15. Vivien Lowenstein 'Arts Review'. 6/7/79.

16. Richard Walker 'Arts Review'. 9/11/79.

17. Letter Caroline Portway to Mary Lambert. 30/1/79.

18. Julie Lacey 'Arts Review'. 11/4/80.

19. Julie Lacey 'Arts Review'. 4/7/80.

20. Frances Spalding 'Arts Review'. 29/2/80.

Chapter Six

1. Marjorie Parr to Peter Thursby. 9/10/74.

2. Bernice Sandelson in conversation with the author, London. 3/5/07.

3. Robert Sandelson 'The Independent'. 10/7/92.

4. Jilly Knight in telephone conversation with the author. 1/6/08.

5. Tim Boon in telephone conversation with the author. 2/7/08.

6. Parr to Thursby. 11/11/87.

7. Vivien ap Rhys Pryce with the author, Marlborough. 19/7/08.

8. Aart van Kruiselbergen in conversation with the author, London. 30/7/07.

9. Evelyn Williams e-mail to Mary Lambert. 23/5/07.

10. Leslie Waddington. Letter to the author. 28/3/07.

11. David Michie. Letter to the author. 7/7/08.

12. David Evans. Letter to the author. July 08.

13. Nick Leigh in conversation with the author, Marlborough. 19/7/08.

14. Mo and Alan Gise. Letter to Mary Lambert. 9/7/08.

15. Dick Allen. Letter to the author. 3/6/07.

16. Nigel Van Wieck e-mail to Mary Lambert. 21/9/08.

Chronological list of Exhibitions held at the Marjorie Parr Gallery

1963
                      Guy Worsdell, Paintings
Mixed exhibition including sculpture by Peter Thursby

1964 August
Mixed exhibition including Sculpture by Peter Ball

September 3-26 — Peter Thursby, Sculpture and Drawings
October 1-24 — John Hitchens, Paintings: Sussex Landscapes

1965
Sculpture by Peter Ball, Roger Leigh and Jill Tweed

May — Guy Worsdell, Paintings
June 2-23 — Margaret Lovell, Sculpture
September 8- 2 October — Peter Thursby, Sculpture and Drawings; and Catherine Yarrow, High fired earth and pastels
November 3-27 — John Hitchens, Paintings: Land, Sea, Sky
December — Small Works for Christmas Gifts

1966 January — Mixed Exhibition
February — Sculpture
April — Mixed Exhibition including Paintings by Patrick Hall, John Hitchens and Kate Nicholson
May — Small Sculpture including work by Robert Clatworthy, Elisabeth Frink, Henry Moore, June Barrington-Ward, Mark Ingram, Margaret Lovell and Marcia Panama
November 9- December 24 — Small Sculpture by:

Kenneth Armitage	R.R. Nele
Lynn Chadwick	Marcia Panama
Elisabeth Frink	Enzo Plazzotta
Mark Ingram	Oliffe Richmond
Margaret Lovell	Peter Thursby
Denis Mitchell	Joe Tilson
	F.E. MacWilliam
	Werthman

1967 February 16-March 11 — John Hitchens, Paintings
March 16-April 29 (Easter) — Mixed Exhibition including sculpture by Enzo Plazzotta
May 4-May 25 — Breon O'Casey, Paintings and Reliefs; Denis Mitchell, Sculpture
July 6-29 — Pottery by:

John Chalke	Pilar Saizar
Janet Leach	Catherine Yarrow

Wall-hangings and Paintings by:

Tadek Beutlich	Thetis Blacker

August 3-26 — Flower Paintings by:

Sonia Akjayan	John Hitchens
Elizabeth Allen	Jean Marchand
Heather Craigmile	Winifred Nicholson
Philippa Denby	Roland Suddaby
Duncan Grant	Guy Worsdell
Patrick Hall	

September 7-30 — Philip Hicks, Metal Reliefs and Paintings; Jill Tweed, Bird Sculpture

October 5-26	Guy Worsdell, Paintings
	Michael Rothenstein, Prints
	Tadek Beultich, Prints

| November 9-December 23 | Small Sculpture by: |

Robert Adams	Mark Ingram
Anton	Margaret Lovell
Barrington Ward	F.E. McWilliam
Brian Bishop	Denis Mitchell
Paul Bridgeman	Marcia Panama
J.C. Collier	Enzo Plazzotta
Elisabeth Frink	Oliffe Richmond
Olaf Graveson	Adam Tessier
	Werthmann

1968

January	Small Paintings
February 1-22	Henri Hayden: Gouaches, Small Oils, Lithographs
March 7-30	Edinburgh College of Art: Paintings by the Lecturers
April 7-30	Edinburgh College of Art: Paintings by the Post Graduate Students
May	MARJORIE BUYS PROPERTY IN ST IVES
June 6-29	Margaret Lovell, Sculpture
July-August	Summer Exhibition: Paintings and Small Sculpture including work by new artists (September 7-28: Second St Ives Group, Exhibition of Paintings, Sculpture and Ceramics at Austin Reed, 103 Regent Street, London W1)
September 5-28	Kate Nicholson, greek epigrams
October 3-26	Enzo Plazzotta, Sculpture
November 7-30	John Hitchens, Paintings
December 5-24	Christmas Exhibition: Small Sculpture

1969

February 6-March 1	Denis Mitchell, Sculpture
March 6-29	Vivien ap Rhys Pryce, Sculpture
	Pier Steensma, Paintings from Nepal
	F.G. Hughes, Perspex and Nylon Constructions
April	Modem Paintings, Sculpture and Pots
April 2	OPENING OF ST IVES GALLERY
May 8-31	James Cumming, Paintings
	also works by other Scottish painters including John Johnstone, David Michie and Robin Philipson
June 5-28	Mark Ingram, Constructions and Sculpture
July 3-August 30	Pottery by: Janet Leach, William Marshall, Michael Truscott, etc.
	Paintings of Pottery: Guy Worsdell
	Mixed Exhibition of Paintings and Sculpture in the Upper Galleries
September 4-27	Thetis Blacker, Paintings and Wall Hangings
	Catherine Yarrow, Pottery
October 2-25	John Milne, Sculpture
	Breon O'Casey, Paintings
October 30-November 22	200 Years of English Watercolours, 1770-1969
November 27-December 24	Small Sculpture and Henri Hayden Gouaches

1970	January	LONDON GALLERY CLOSED FOR RE-DECORATION
	February 5-28	Douglas Portway, Paintings
		Michael Black, Sculpture
	March 5-26	David Evans, Paintings
	April 9-May 2	Peter Eugene Ball, Primitive Sculpture
		Pauline Kray, Hinterglas Paintings
		John Piper, Lithograph and Silk Screen Prints
	May 7-30	Jeff Hoare, Paintings
		Robert Scott Simon, Clocks/Sculpture
	June 4-27	Margaret Lovell, Sculpture
	July 9-August 29	Ceramics and Sculpture for out-of-doors
	September 10-October 3	Kate Nicholson, Paintings from Tunisia
		Jupp Dembach-Mayen, Sculpture and Reliefs
	October 8-31	Pottery by:

Bernard Leach   Lucie Rie
William Marshall   Catherine Yarrow
James Campbell   Ewen Henderson
Hans Coper   Janet Leach
and Patrick Hall, Watercolour Paintings 1968-70

	November 5-28	John Hitchens, Paintings: Sussex, Scotland, Wales
	December 4-24	Christmas exhibition: Small Sculpture and Kinetics, Painting, Pottery
1971	January 8-30	Nigel Van Wieck
		Kinetics - Perspex + Light
	February 5-7	James Cumming: Recent Paintings
	March 5-27	Peter Thursby, Sculpture, 1969-1971
		Betty Holman, Paintings
	April 2-24	Bernard Leach, Pottery
		Donatienne Sapriel, Paintings in Japanese Ink
	May 7-9	Paintings, Drawings, Etchings, Lithographs
		Yankel Adler, Elisabeth Frink, Henri Hayden, Jean Helion, Barbara Hepworth, Ben Nicholson, Victor Pasmore, John Piper etc.
	June 11-July 3	W. Barns-Graham, Paintings
		Marcia Panama, Sculpture
	July 8-August 28	Chelsea in the 19th Century: Greaves, Whistler, Roussel, also Sculpture for out-of-doors by Gallery Artists (27 July: Third St Ives Group Exhibition at Austin Reed, 103 Regent Street, London W1, opened by Sir Norman Reid, Director of the Tate Gallery) DURING 1971 MARJORIE PARR SELLS HER ST IVES GALLERY TO MR AND MRS PETER GIBBS OF CHELTENHAM
	September 10-October	Thetis Blacker, Batik Paintings
	October 8-30	Denis Mitchell, Recent Sculpture 1969-71
	November 5-27	Douglas Portway, Paintings
	December 3-27	Paintings and Sculpture for Christmas Presents
1972	January 7-29	Jesse Watkins, Steel Sculpture
	February 4-26	Peter Eugene Ball, Primitive Sculpture
	March 3-25	Jeff Hoare, Recent Paintings. (Artists from Marjorie Parr, Austin Reed, Regent Street).
	April 7-29	John Milne, Sculpture
	May 4-27	David Evans, Paintings

June 9-July 1	Chelsea and Kensington in the 18th and 19th Centuries Greaves, Whistler, and other artists of the period	
July 7-9	Janet Leach, Pottery; and in the Upper Gallery, Paintings by Bryan Illsley and Tony O'Malley	
August 4-26	Paintings, Sculpture & Pottery by Gallery Artists	
September 8-30	Margaret Lovell, Sculpture - Bronze, Slate, Marble	
October 6-28	John Hitchens, Recent Landscape Paintings	
November 3-25	Nigel Van Wieck, Kinetics - Perspex + Light Large works with electronic music by Richard Rodney Bennett shown in the Austin Reed Gallery, 4th Floor, 103 Regent Street, London W1; Smaller works shown in the Marjorie Parr Gallery	
December 1-23	Patrick Hall, Watercolour Paintings, 1970-72	

1973 January 3-20 — Primitive Paintings and Sculpture; also Kinetics, Sculpture, Paintings and Pottery by Gallery Artists

January 26- February 24	John Piper, Paintings and Graphics
March 2-24	Anne Redpath, R.S.A., Paintings and Drawings
April 6-28	John Christopherson, Paintings; and Bernard Leach, Pottery
May 10-June2	James Cumming, Paintings
June 8-30	Tom Davison, Recent Paintings
July 6-28	Ewen Henderson, Pottery and Watercolours; Elena Gaputyte, Sculpture and Drawings
August 2-September 1	Evelyn Williams, Reliefs and Wax Sculpture; on the 1st and 2nd Floors: Paintings, Sculpture, Pottery; also Prints and Drawings of Old Chelsea
September 7-29	Jessica Dismorr, Paintings 1920-30; and Aart van Kruiselbergen, Recent Paintings
October 5-27	In the place of a postponed Thetis Blacker exhibition the work of the following artists was shown:

Lyn Chadwick	Henry Moore
Cecil Collins	Ben Nicholson
Elisabeth Frink	Victor Pasmore
Henri Hayden	John Piper
Barbara Hepworth	Anne Redpath
Ivon Hitchens	William Roberts
Andre Masson	Graham Sutherland

November 2-24	Douglas Portway, Oils on Canvas and Paper
November 30- December 22	Phyllis Mackenzie, The Legal Scene

1974 January — Paintings and Sculpture by Gallery Artists

February 1-23	Enzo Plazzotta, Sculpture
March 1-23	Noel Counihan, Australian Realist Paintings
March 29-April 27	Jeff Hoare, Paintings
May 3-25	Peter Eugene Ball, Sculpture; also on the First Floor, John Banting, oils, watercolours and drawings
June 7-29	Anthony Twentyman, large and small sculpture in stone, slate, bronze and wood; also Patricia Allen, Persian Paintings and Animals

July 1	MARJORIE PARR SELLS THE KING'S ROAD GALLERY TO MR DAVID GILBERT, BUT CONTINUES TO WORK WITH HIM UNTIL DECEMBER 1975	
July 5-August 31	Gouaches, Watercolours, Drawings by	
	Elisabeth Frink	Sidney Nolan
	Henry Hayden	Victor Pasmore
	Ivon Hitchens	John Piper
	Fernand Leger	Anne Redpath
	Henry Moore	William Roberts
	Ben Nicholson	Graham Sutherland
	Also Graphics by the above artists and other contemporaries	
September 6-28	David Evans, Paintings; also Geoffrey Eastop, Ceramic wall-hangings and dishes	
October 4-26	John Milne, Sculpture and Drawings (large work was shown in the Rectory Garden, Old Church Street, Chelsea)	
November 1-23	Eardley Knollys, Recent Paintings	
November 29- December 21	Patrick Hall, Watercolour Paintings 1972-74; in the Lower Gallery, Andrew Lanyon, Paintings; also Recent Pottery by Gallery Artists	

1975 January	Paintings and Sculpture by Gallery artists	
February 7-1 March	John Christopherson: 'The Obsessive Image'; also Dick Onians, Carvings in wood and stone, with Wall Hangings by Eta Ingham-Mohrhardt	
March 7-29	Aart van Kruiselbergen, Recent Paintings; (in conjunction with an exhibition of his work opening on the same day at the Cricklewood Art Centre, Aldgate, South Australia); On the First and Second Floors: Sculpture and Drawings including work by:	
	Robert Adams	Eli Ilan
	June Barrington Ward	Geraldine Knight
	Lynn Chadwick	Margaret Lovell
	Ann Christopher	F.E. McWilliam
	Ernst Eisenmayer	Vivien ap Rhys Pryce
	Michael Gillespie	Janos Stryk
		Jesse Watkins
	also Sculpture Clocks by Robert Scott Simon	
April 4-26	Shlomo Cassos, Paintings and Tapestries; In the Lower Gallery: Ewen Henderson, Recent Paintings	
May 2-24	Denis Mitchell, Sculpture In the Lower Gallery: Edward Piper, Drawing and Paintings	
May 30-June 21	Angelica Garnett, Pastels; and James Hussey, Paintings	
July 4-August 30	Scottish Paintings and Drawings 1775-1975: A Summer Exhibition of work by Scottish Artists past and present..........	
September 5-27	Tom Davison, Recent Paintings; In the Lower Gallery: Ruth Neeman, Enamel and Mixed Media Paintings	
October 3-25	Enzo Plazzotta, Figurative Bronze Sculpture; in the Lower Gallery: Eardley Knollys, Works on Paper	

	October 31- November 22	Douglas Portway, Oils on Canvas and Paper; in the Lower Gallery: Luis Canizares, Tempera and Ink Drawings
	November 28- December 20	Christian Brett, Landscape and Still-Life Paintings and Drawings; and Robert Scott Simon, Sculpture and Sculpture Clocks
1976	January 3-31	Paintings, Sculpture and Drawings 1920-1975
	January 29-Febuary 1	British Luxury Fair, Dubai
	February 6-28	Peter Eugene Ball, Primitive Sculpture and Pier Steensma, Sleep, an Indian theme and other recent works on paper In the Lower Gallery: Mixed Exhibition including the paintings of Margaret Neve
	March 5-27	James Cumming, Paintings 1976; In the Lower Gallery: Betty Cumming, Tapestries
	April 2-24	John Hitchens, Landscape Series and Flowers; In the Lower Gallery: Andrew Walsh, Paintings
	April 30-May 22	Jane B. Armstrong, Animal Sculpture in stone; and Philippa Denby, Recent Oil Paintings
	May 28-June 19	John Piper, Paintings, Graphics and Ceramics
	June 16-21	International Art Fair, Basel, Switzerland with Paintings by Douglas Portway and Sculpture by Peter Eugene Ball
	June 25-July 17	Dorothy Girouard, Happy Birthdays and other Paintings; and Ewen Henderson, Recent Pottery and Greek Paintings
	July 23-September 4	European Paintings, Drawings and Graphics; and New Work by Gallery Artists, including Water Sculpture by Fleischmann
	September 10- October 2	Christine Fox, Sculpture; and Manuel Menan, Colour Etchings
	October 8-30	Thelma Hulbert, Recent Paintings; and Michel Kuipers, Ceramic Sculpture and Porcelain
	November 5-27	Jeff Hoare, Paintings; David Backhouse, Sculpture
	December 3-24	Patrick Hall, Watercolour Paintings 1974-1976
1977	January	Paintings and Sculpture by Gallery artists
	February 18- March 12	Lee Brews, Oil and Mixed Media Paintings; and Yolanda Sonnabend, Drawings for Stage Designs
	March	THE GALLERY NAME IS CHANGED TO GILBERT PARR GALLERY
	March 18-April 9	John Hitchens, Flower Paintings; also Avinash Chandra, Recent Paintings
	April 15-May 7	Michael Gillespie, Bronze Sculpture; also Bernard Stern, Recent Ink Washes
	May 13-June 4	Patricia Allen, Paintings, 1976-77; also John Bond, Beachscapes; also Paul Fowler, Recent Paintings
	June 10-July 9	David Evans, Paintings
	July-August	Paintings and Sculpture by Gallery artists
	September 9- October 1	Barcelo, Gouache and Ink Paintings; also Barbara Rae, Paintings

	October 7-19	Peter Eugene Ball, Sculpture; also Shlomo Cassos, Oil Pastels and Etchings
	November 4-26	Douglas Portway, Oils on Canvas and Paper; also Richard Blomfield, Structures and Situations
	December 2-24	Margaret Neve, Paintings; also Ivo Mosley, Pots
1978	January	Paintings and Sculpture by Gallery Artists
	February 17-March 11	Pier Steensma, Watercolours from India and Tunisia
	March 17-April 15	Glyn Morgan, Paintings, Collages, Drawings
	April 21-May 13	John Milne, Sculpture; also Bryon Temple, Pottery; and Geoffrey MacEwan, Watercolours
	May 25-June 24	Norah Glover, Recent Paintings
	June 30-July 22	Michael Wharton, Paintings
	August & September	Paintings & Drawings of Distinction 1951-1978
	October 6-28	Andrew Lanyon, Paintings, Collages, Drawings; Christine Fox, Sculpture, New works in bronze and aluminium
	November 3-25	James Campbell, Ceramics; also Neil Dallas Brown, Drawings and Paintings
	December 1-23	Patrick Hall, Watercolour Paintings 1976-1978
1979	January 25-March 3	Antonio Mari Ribas, India Ink Drawings
	February 8-March 3	Lee Brews, Paintings; also Michael Gillespie, Bronze Sculpture;
	March 8-31	John Emanual, The Nude - Recent Paintings
	April	Sculpture and Paintings by Gallery Artists
	May 4-26	John Bond, Beachscapes and Landscapes; also Will Maclean, Boxed Constructions and Drawings
	June 7-July 7	John Hitchens, Paintings
	July 12-September	Figurative Paintings, Drawings and Sculpture of Distinction
	September 20-October 20	Peter Eugene Ball, Sculpture; also Jan Hubertus, 'Meditations' - Paintings in Tempera and Watercolour
	October 25-November 17	Douglas Portway, Recent Works
	November 22-December 15	Margaret Neve, Paintings in oil on wood panels; also Ivo Mosley, Pots
1980	January & February	Sculpture and Paintings by Gallery Artists
	March 21-April 19	Glyn Morgan, Paintings and Collages
	April 25-May 17	Richard Blomfield, Drawings, Paintings and Sculptures 1977-1980
	June 25-July 19	David Evans New Paintings and Drawings
	August & September	Sculpture and Paintings by Gallery Artists
	October 3-25	Valerie Thornton, Columns and Windows; Michael Chase, Forest Interiors
	November 28-December 20	Pier Steensma, Watercolours
1981	Records are incomplete for this year and for 1982	
	October 2-24	Patrick Hall, Watercolour Paintings 1978-1981
	October 30-November 21	Douglas Portway, Paintings
1982	March 12-April 3	Clive Soord, Ceramics - The Master of the Dragons

David Gilbert closed the Gallery in October 1982 and moved to the Black Forest, Germany where he and his wife, Inga, continued to promote the work of living artists, in particular Peter Eugene Ball, Paul Fowler, Barry Herbert, Jan Hubertus, Will MacLean, Douglas Portway and Lucie Rie from their new address, Steinbachstrasse 14, D-7891 Remetschwiel, Sudschwarzwald, West Germany. He continued to exhibit work at Art Fairs.

Index

Acknowledgements

We are very grateful to the many people who have helped with the production of this book. We would particularly like to thank Marjorie's family, Leslie and Sheila Mary Pollard, Mark, Simon and Ian Pollard for providing information about Marjorie's early life, and for the photograph of the drawing of Marjorie by Alfred Hitchens; also for access to Marjorie's personal photograph albums of the Gallery, from where many photographs have come, especially of the St Ives period.

We also acknowledge with thanks, the help we have received from the following people who have either given of their time to be interviewed, or have provided photographs of items from their collections. This book could not have been written without them: Jill Tweed, Philip Hicks, Jeff Hoare, Aart van Kruisel-bergen, Bernice Sandelson, Margaret Lovell, Vivien ap Rhys Pryce, John Hitchens, Margaret Neve and Breon O'Casey gave interviews. Former staff members like Ebe Wharton, Jilly Knight, Pat Gelley Sargent and Tim Boon provided useful information based on direct, working experience of the gallery's heyday. One of them, Mary Lambert, commissioned the book an provided crucial archivel material and full support to the extent that this volume owes everything to her. The collector Dick Allen provided hospitality and insights about doing business with Marjorie Parr. His son Charles took some excellent photos of work from the Allen collection. Harley Carpenter, Nick Leigh, Keith Chapman, Joe Calvert and Andrew Lanyon also provided photos. Leslie Waddington, David Evans, David Michie, Barbara Rae, Peter and Mo Thursby and Andrew Lanyon responded by letter providing useful insights. Michael Shepherd wrote an illuminating Foreword. The staff of the Old Bakehouse were as always a pleasure to work with. Peter Archer, the painter, provided hospitality in Abertillery. Simon Bishop, musician and graphic designer in Bristol, designed the covers.

Further thanks go to Robert Sandelson and Irving Grose for providing all-important launches at their respective London and St Ives galleries. Thanks also to Anthony Beeson of Bristol Central Library and the estate and family of Enzo Plazzotta. Toni Carver of the 'St Ives Times and Echo' supported and helped set up a lecture on Marjorie Parr by the author during the St Ives September Festival. Finally thanks to Pam and Rodney Giesler, Alan and Mo Gise, Jim Knight, Henrietta Ryan, Gillian Raffles, Anthony Shaw, Sheila Sorley and Trevor Barratt and, on the home front, Maggie Davies and Ben Harcourt.